GETTING STARTED IN BALLET

GETTING STARTED IN BALLET

A Parent's Guide to Dance Education

. . .

Anna Paskevska

NEW YORK   OXFORD

Oxford University Press

1997

Oxford University Press

Oxford   New York
Athens   Auckland   Bangkok   Bogotá   Bombay
Buenos Aires   Calcutta   Cape Town   Dar es Salaam
Delhi   Florence   Hong Kong   Istanbul   Karachi
Kuala Lumpur   Madras   Madrid   Melbourne
Mexico City   Nairobi   Paris   Singapore
Taipei   Tokyo   Toronto   Warsaw

and associated companies in
Berlin   Ibadan

Published by Oxford University Press, Inc.,
198 Madison Avenue, New York, New York 10016

Oxford is a registered trademark of Oxford University Press

Library of Congress Cataloging-in Publication Data
Paskevska, Anna.
Getting started in ballet : a parent's guide to dance education /
by Anna Paskevska.
p.   cm.
Includes bibliographical references and index.
ISBN 0-19-511716-6 (cloth). — ISBN 0-19-511717-4 (pbk)
1. Ballet — Study and teaching.   2. Dance schools.   I. Title.
GV1788.5.P377   1997   97-18849

FRONTISPIECE:
Students of the Chicago Academy for the Arts
©1997 Mitchell Canoff

1 3 5 7 9 8 6 4 2
Printed in the United States of America on acid-free paper

To my family, Boris, Tamela and Tatiana, Theo,
Linda and little Theo and Brianna, and
my daughter Nadezhda

Contents

Preface

THIS informative book by Anna Paskevska is invaluable for every would-be dancer. The author claims it was written for parents but, as a dancer myself, I know there must also be a parent within every successful performer guiding the developing body, mind, and spirit. Of course, the support of parents and teachers is also a necessity, so this intelligent and informed book is for everyone with any interest in dance as a career.

All of the glimpses of personal experience which reveal the author: her knowledge of dancers of the past and the present and their accomplishments, her life as a student and performer in the Paris Opera Ballet and later as a teacher with her own school make interesting reading. Her penetration and insight into correct procedure and problems along the way are what every parent and student needs to know.

Finally, through the writing of this book, it is Anna Paskevska herself who becomes the parent sharing her experience, her intelligent advice, and her caring mind and heart with all parents of students and all would-be dancers. And I advise every one of them to read this common sense and inspiring picture of a dancer's life.

Sybil Shearer

Foreword

BECOMING a dancer, a lifetime quest, involves more than talent, desire, and discipline. These are the stones for the building of a house. They remain only that unless there is a structure, and that cannot be accomplished without a design. "Getting Started in Ballet" is a book intended to assist in the design of a dancer's life. Like a knowledgeable architect, Mrs. Paskevska speaks to us about the issues and concerns in the creation of that course, so that dancers, or anyone involved with the guidance of a dancer, can make informed decisions each step of the way.

"Getting Started in Ballet" is an invaluable source book. Using her knowledge and inspirations based on a life in dance, professionally and personally, Mrs. Paskevska guides us developmentally through matters crucial to a dancer's full realization. She does this with information that is backed up by academic research and personal anecdotes.

A true cornerstone towards a celestial architecture, I found "Getting Started in Ballet" informative and enjoyable.

Violette Verdy

Introduction

Y OU WANT to take your child to a dance class, where do you go? How do you know that the school listed in the yellow pages will be suitable? Which type of classes will be most beneficial? Because dancers need to be trained from an early age, the parents' choice of a first teacher, and the advice and support through the long years of training are central to their development. Even if neither the child nor the parents envision dance as a profession but simply look for a meaningful extracurricular activity, the choices need to be guided by some knowledge of the field.

The perceived glamor of the dance profession is seldom matched by its realities. It is both more exciting and more demanding than anyone standing on the outside can apprehend. It is exciting, not because of the gala occasions, but in subtle and personal ways — feeling the total stretch of a leg, experiencing the headiness of multiple turns, arriving at a level of technique when the motion takes over and step follows step without conscious effort or mental deliberation. And it is demanding because dance possesses the dancer. As children we give up our social life to attend classes and rehearsals and put up with aching muscles and blistered feet. As professionals we persevere knowing that there are few material rewards, little security and continued physical discomfort. Thus it is a life that cannot be imposed but can be anticipated by proper training and awareness of the hazards.

Through the thirty years of my teaching career, parents have asked a multitude of questions, from "when will my daughter be ready to do pointe?" to "she has lost a lot of weight, what can we do?" In these pages, I endeavor to answer these concerns and offer an overview of the world of dance.

GETTING STARTED IN BALLET

.

Students from the Academy of Movement
and Music in Oak Park, Illinois.
©1997 Mitchell Canoff

✻ 1 ✻

Why Dance?

FOR HUMAN BEINGS, dancing is as natural as breathing. We have forgotten how our ancestors danced or why they danced, but children remember. My granddaughter at six months would stop crawling and begin rocking as soon as she heard music. A conversation with prospective students' parents frequently begins: "Jenny is always dancing, around the kitchen, in the living room. . . ." How old is Jenny? Typically she is about two or three.

Why do we dance? There is no single answer to cover all reasons. In the past, humankind danced in worship and celebration. In the Western tradition, social dance has occupied a very special place: we dance for the pleasure it gives us. The tradition of classical ballet has its roots in the social dances at the courts of the European kings. We dance to entertain others, or we dance to share our feelings or the feelings of the role we portray. At a more pedestrian level, we dance because it is a good exercise. We learn to dance to promote good posture, to burn off calories, to become more graceful. All of the above reasons have one factor in common — through the act of dance we experience a sense of communality. We share or communicate our sense of well-being through motion.

When Isadora Duncan was asked when she started dancing, she replied, "In the womb." Martha Graham said that she did not choose to dance; dance chose her. Indeed, dance is seldom a conscious decision; when the time comes to make a commitment to serious training, the dance is in the blood of those who have been chosen. To stop dancing seems as inconceivable as to stop breathing.

Although not everyone is born to be a professional dancer, dance training benefits all. It establishes an awareness of the body, and an appreciation for what the body can do. It also aids in the physical and mental development of the child.

A study conducted by William Greenough at the University of Illinois has linked the development of synaptic connections in the brain to simple physical tasks repeated many times. "When you exercise vigorously and regularly, you are not only changing your muscles . . . you are changing your brain. . . . Improving the brain's ability to respond efficiently to one form of exercise also prepares it to better handle other types of physical activities" (*Chicago Tribune*, 1991). Greenough suggests that exercise is good because it enlarges the brain's capacity to respond to a variety of stimuli: "When the environment demands extensive repetition of a small set of simple, well practiced movements, the vascular support is altered to handle the increased metabolic load and is associated with higher levels of neural activity".

A long accepted treatment for mentally impaired children is patterning, which involves teaching the child basic motions (such as crawling) by manipulating the limbs. This treatment is said to stimulate the brain into patterns that are essential for the child's normal development. Although no scientific study to date supports this claim, parents have often told me that their child's ability to learn and concentrate improved after they started dance classes.

Dance is also of great benefit in the social sphere. Children in a dance class become aware of spatial relationships and learn how to work in harmony with each other. In this noncompetitive environment they learn about cooperation and support of each other's efforts. In creative-movement or pre-ballet classes, they also learn how to express their ideas and imaginings, thereby improving their communication skills.

Dance teaches discipline — not the kind that is imposed on us, but a deep-rooted response, an innate need for orderliness and harmony. Appreciation of the visual arts, both sculpture and painting, is spurred by dance training; dance aids recognition of form, balance and, line. Dance also encourages an awareness of the rhythm in all of life and our participation in that rhythm. Bertram Ross, a principal member of Martha Graham's company and a teacher at her school in New York, exclaimed during one class: "Go to the country, go to the park, take your shoes off, and run through the grass!" He was urging us to reconnect with nature in order to understand the movement he was demonstrating. Animals in the wild do not overeat or oversleep; they live in harmony with their nature. It could be argued that a lack of discipline is a sign of unbalance, or, conversely, that a balanced life is a disciplined life. When we are not in harmony with our nature, it is as if we close the door to our inner promptings. We stay up too late at night, feel groggy in the morning, drink too much coffee, and then are wired up and prone to rash decisions and fits of temper. We are out of balance and act in an undisciplined manner. Go to the country, take your shoes off, and feel the grass caressing your toes — or go to a dance class!

Much has been written about the "high" that runners experience after a vigorous race. In a subtler and, I like to think, a more complete way, dancers also experience a transcendent sensation. After a good class, all worries seem manageable, all problems solvable. During a difficult period in my life, my mother once said to me as I was leaving for class, "Go seek your oblivion." She was not wrong, although at the time I felt she was unjust. Class provided me solace and grounding; in class I had a measure of control, and the physical exertion was in itself cleansing. It was also cheaper than a psychiatrist!

At the arts high school where I teach, the dance students are the most disciplined members of the community. Typically, they have a high grade-point average, are responsible about handing in their homework on time, and are courteous and considerate. They form a close, but not closed, community and are supportive of each other. Although some will not pursue a career in dance after graduation, all invest a maximum of effort in their technical improvement and their understanding of the art form.

The Greeks knew the value of dance; not only did they dance in worship and ritual, but they also made dance a part of the training of athletes and warriors. Through exercise comes control and awareness, and through control comes a heightened sense of physicality, coordination, and grace. In the heyday of the European Renaissance, all of Europe danced, and its courts laid the foundation of today's ballet. After the dark Medieval era, when asceticism, self-denial, self-flagellation, and hairshirts had been thought to bring one closer to God, humankind was again free to extol the pleasure of well-being through movement. Later, at the seventeenth-century French court of Louis XIV, courtly manners were polished through the study of dance and deportment. In 1661, Louis established the Académie Royale de la Danse, thus marking the beginning of the separation between professionals and amateurs. Technique developed and was codified, a sophisticated notation system was developed, and treatises on training were written.

Dance training has also become popular in our age of heightened awareness of physical fitness. Many people either take up dancing for the first time or return to it in their adulthood. They appreciate the toning and control that dance fosters, enjoy the soothing predictability of the lesson, and can let their imaginations soar to the rhythms of the classical music of the ballet class or the driving pulse of a modern or jazz class.

HISTORICAL OVERVIEW

Of the four theatrical dance styles we will be discussing, ballet is the first to have developed training methods. The rules of the classical ballet technique are based on the motions that are natural to human beings. For example, when we walk, as the right foot comes forward the left arm swings forward. From this natural motion came ballet's law of opposition. Balance and the need to maximize the push off the floor in jumps made us appreciate how the weight of the body affects all motion. This knowledge resulted in dancers' associating positions of the head and arms with specific postures or movements of the legs in order to facilitate or counterbalance motions. The use of turnout came about when it was discovered that turning out the toes allowed for a variety of steps to be executed that were otherwise either impossible or ungainly, such as the entrechats, a jump where the legs bypass each other in a rapid beating motion. Louis XIV is reputed to have mastered the entrechats six (the legs bypass each other twice during the jump). A popular explanation for the renaming of the entrechats trois, a single beating of the legs, is that when Louis could no longer perform the more difficult entrechat six, the entrechats trois became known as "royale" in order not to offend the king. The early technique focused on intricate footwork accompanied by graceful movements in the upper body, head, and arms.

Costumes into the eighteenth century were rather cumbersome, as they followed the fashion of the day. Marie Camargo (1710–1770) scandalized her public by shortening her skirt to reveal her ankle and thus show off the cabrioles and entrechats that she has mastered. These steps had hitherto been performed only by male dancers, whose costumes permitted a fuller view of the body as well as a broader range of motion. Camargo's rebellious gesture has assured her place in the history books, but more importantly, she opened the door for female dancers to experience the whole breadth of the technique.

During the eighteenth century, dance's vocabulary of motion relied on the steps used in court dances. Dance teachers experimented with movement to find new steps or sequences, which they then used in the composition of dances. Dancers were often their own choreographers, and they favored steps in which they excelled. For example, if a dancer pirouetted easily, he or she practiced turns and incorporated them into his or her compositions, utilizing them more than other motions; thus dancers became known for specific feats. As dance steps increased in complexity, the gap between the vocabulary of the court dances and professional dance widened, and the need to train dancers was felt. A vocabulary for training developed, and exercises involving the barre developed as a prelude for work in the center, which became the basis for a choreographic vocabulary.

Renowned dancer Carlo Blasis (1797–1878) was considered the most influential teacher of his day. In 1828 he published *The Code of Terpsichore*, a treatise on the art of dancing. In this book Blasis outlines several types of motions still performed today, and discusses the function of the exercises in limbering up for performance. These exercises form the base of the classical ballet technique.

By the romantic era, from the 1820s, all dancers underwent this training regimen. Marie Taglioni (1804–1884), the epitome of the romantic ballerina, was taught by her father, Filippo Taglioni (1777–1871). She often fainted from exhaustion by the end of the two-hour classes that he devised for her.

Ethereality and lightness were some of the essential characteristics of a romantic ballerina. In order to enhance those qualities, female dancers began to rise fleetingly on their toes. From this physical innovation the pointe shoe developed, with its hard block to protect the toes and its pliable, yet strong, inner sole to support the arch. By the second half of the nineteenth century, dancing on pointe had become an important facet of the ballerina's technique.

Ballet technique is ultimately adaptable to the character of the people performing it. Thus, in the late nineteenth century, Italian dancers were known for their speed and dexterity in turning, the French for their nobility, the Danish for the lightness of their jumps. Ballet masters of the nineteenth century traveled extensively, which accounts for the dissemination of ballet technique as well as its basic homogeneity. This tradition of travel has persisted to our day, ensuring the continued sharing of ideas and making dancers true citizens of the world.

Russia had long admired the arts of Western Europe, especially those of the French. Russia routinely imported dancing masters both to teach at the Imperial School and to produce ballets. The man credited with the rise and preeminence of the Russian ballet is Marius Petipa (1818–1910), who came to Russia in 1847 as a dancer and was appointed ballet master and choreographer in 1862. He held the position of choreographer until his retirement in 1903. Under his leadership, the foundation of the classical repertory was established, and the rules and usages of the ballet vocabulary were firmly fixed. Two more notable styles influenced the emergence of the Russian style: the Danish School, represented by Christian Johannsson (1817–1903), who, after a distinguished dancing career, became chief teacher at the Mariynski in 1860; and the Italian School, represented by Enrico Cecchetti (1850–1928), who taught in Russia from 1892. One of the distinguishing features of Russian folk dancing is the expressiveness of the arms and upper body. This feature was incorporated into the balletic vocabulary and gave the Russian style its particular character. Because expressiveness of the upper body relies on the strength and flexibility of the torso, the basic exercises practiced in class needed to address this issue. Nicolai Legat (1869–1937), teacher and theorist, embodied this blending of styles upon which the Russian School is based. Later, Agrippina Vaganova (1879–1951) based the method of teaching in Russian schools on Legat's theories.

In 1908, the Russian impresario Serge Diaghilev (1872–1929) brought to Paris the production of the opera *Boris Godunov* by Mussorgsky. The overwhelming success of this production led to successive Russian seasons in Paris. Although the initial season featured opera, not ballet, the French public was especially impressed with the dancers whom Diaghilev had assembled from the ranks of the Mariynsky and Bolshoi ballets, including Vaslav Nijinsky and Tamara Karsavina. Both Cecchetti and Legat were employed at different times as ballet masters for Diaghilev's company. Les Ballets Russes de Diaghilev, as the company was eventually known, was the instrument by which interest in dance was rekindled in the West, leading to a renaissance of the art form not only in Europe but in the United States as well.

Previously, toward the end of the nineteenth century in Europe, dance had experienced a decline. Ballet had become a frivolous display that relied more on the charm and youth of the dancers to attract the public than on artistic merit. Some artists rebelled against what they perceived as ballet's stultification, denouncing it as mere form with no content. Isadora Duncan (1878–1927) dared to dance barefoot in a light tunic that allowed her to move freely and revealed the lines of her body, and she developed her own expressive style of movement. Although Duncan did not attract American audiences at the beginning of her career, Europe, especially Germany and Russia, welcomed and admired her. Her ideas prompted a reevaluation of the established practices in the dance world, and she greatly influenced a young choreographer at the Imperial School, Mikhail Fokine (1880–1942). In his approach to ballet choreography, Fokine became highly critical of the three-act ballets so popular during Petipa's tenure. He sought a freer use of the classical technique, and he was able to express his bold ideas as the first choreographer of Diaghilev's innovative productions.

By the beginning of the twentieth century, classical ballet was putting down roots in American soil. Anna Pavlova (1881–1931) introduced audiences to the art form by touring extensively in both South and North America from 1911. Ballet schools were established in Philadelphia, Chicago, and New York in the early part of the century. In 1934 George Balanchine (1904–1983) started the famous School for American Ballet in New York, and at about the same time Ninette de Valois (b. 1898) formed what was to become the Royal Ballet.

During the same period, modern dance emerged as an idea whose time had come. In both the United States and Germany, dancers began to experiment with the new movement fostered by Duncan's work. They turned their backs on the constraints of ballet technique, feeling that dance should express emotions and ideas without resorting to stereotyped gestures. The German artist Mary Wigman (1886–1973) had a great impact on American modern dance through her pupil Hanya Holm (1893–1992), who came to New York in 1931 and nurtured generations of modern dancers. In 1915 in Los Angeles, Ruth St. Denis (1879–1968) and Ted Shawn (1891–1972) opened a school dedicated to the study of their style of modern dance, and started a company known as Denishawn. St. Denis was greatly influenced by Eastern dance, and her choreographic choices reflected that interest. In 1933 Shawn broke from the partnership and established an all-male dance troupe, which toured extensively and was instrumental in overcoming the prejudice against male dancers. Many of the future innovators of modern dance studied at Denishawn and danced in the company. These include Martha Graham (1899–1991), Doris Humphrey (1895–1958), and Charles Weidman (1901–1975). When Graham formed her own company, she began to develop a training method to support her choreographic ideas. Her central concept was Contraction and Release as the initiator for all action. Her movements were often angular and percussive, and her early works were influenced by Freudian symbolism and mythology. Doris Humphrey based her approach to movement on Fall and Recovery; her dances were often fluid and ecstatic. In 1928 Humphrey and Weidman formed their own company, for which Weidman created many works, mostly in a light satirical vein.

These early pioneers spawned a new generation of dancers who shaped the profile of modern dance to our day. Among them were Jose Limon (1908–1972), who had a lifelong association with Humphrey, and Merce Cunningham (b.1919), who danced with Martha Graham before forming his own company in 1952, where he was able to work out his own style of isolated movement in often aleatory compositions. The second generation of innovators included Alwin Nikolais (1912–1993), Eric Hawkins (1909–1995), Sybil Shearer (b.1918), Murray Louis (b.1926), and Paul Taylor (b.1930). These were categorized as nonliteral choreographers. Nikolais and Murray formed the Louis-Nikolais Dance Theatre Lab and produced many experimental works, their central premise being that "the province of art is to explore the inner mechanisms and extra dimensional areas of life."[1] Eric Hawkins, a leading dancer in Martha Graham's company, broke away to form a partnership with the musician Lucia Dlugoszewski. Together they created many dances based on Hawkins's philosophy of the immediacy of experience: dance happens in the now. Shearer danced with the Humphrey-Weidman company and eventually settled in Illinois, where she established a studio and theatre. She created highly individualist works that relied on dynamic action coupled with a serene minimalism of motion. Paul Taylor studied modern dance with Graham and Limon, and ballet with Anthony Tudor and Margaret Craske. His choreography is eclectic; it can be totally nonliteral and then verge on the classical, but it is always highly dynamic.

The list of innovative twentieth-century choreographers is too long to complete here. However, we cannot stop before mentioning Twyla Tharp (1942–) who studied with Graham, Nikolais, Cunningham, and Taylor. Her choreography is performed by major ballet as well as modern-dance companies, and she had a fruitful association with Mikhail Baryshnikov (b.1948) during his tenure as artistic director of the American Ballet Theatre.

To this day, modern dance encourages individualistic expression. Although many innovators established a recognized technique, mod-

1. Murray Louis, "The Contemporary Dance Theatre of Alwin Nikolais," *Dance Observer* 27:1 (Jan. 1960), 5–6.

ern-dance choreographers often break away from their mentors to discover their own way of moving and to build a personal vocabulary of choreographic movement.

· · ·

Jazz dance is considered a truly American expression; it has its origins in the dances of African slaves in America. Despite the Slave Law of 1740, which forbade the playing of drums as well as other instruments, the slaves continued to dance. They adapted to the law by accompanying their dances with clapping hands and banjos as well as the sounds of stamping or shuffling feet. Tap dancing developed from these rhythms. The Irish clog dancers who came to America in the middle of the nineteenth century adopted this tapping and modified it with their own rhythmic combinations. Tap dancing has recently enjoyed a revival thanks to actor/dancer Gregory Hines and Savion Glover, the Tony Award–winning choreographer of *Bring In Da Noise, Bring In Da Funk*. Early pioneers of jazz dance included Bill "Bojangles" Robinson (1878–1949), the Nicholas brothers, and Honi Coles. Many black concert dancers of this century began their training in modern dance, and as choreographers they were able to return to their roots in the creation of powerfully moving dance works. Among the most notable are Pearl Primus (b.1919), Katherine Dunham (b. 1912), and Alvin Ailey (1931–1990).

Jazz and tap dancing began to appear in films in the 1920s, and both established their supremacy in theatrical entertainments such as the extravaganzas of Busby Berkeley (1895–1976) and the beautiful dances choreographed by Agnes de Mille (1909–1993) for musical-theatre productions such as *Oklahoma* (1943). Fred Astaire (1899–1987) is probably the most admired performer of tap dance. His elegant style and exquisite subtleties set the example for the many dancers who followed in his footsteps, like Gene Kelly (1912-1996).

Jazz relies heavily on both classical and modern techniques for the content and sequencing of its warmup exercises, adapting them to reflect its particularities — percussive motions, the use of a broadly opened hand, emphasis on isolation of movement, and a free approach to turn-out (using turned-out or parallel legs as the need arises). Jazz has as many styles as modern dance. It has developed its own warmup exercises, the choice of which usually reflects the bias of the instructor or choreographer. For example, a choreographer whose training was primarily in modern dance will incorporate the concepts of that technique into his or her teaching methods in jazz.

. . .

It is only in the last fifty years (this development was very slow) that dance, including modern dance, has taken on its present athletic profile. Until the 1940s, legs were never lifted above 90 degrees in extensions, and turn-out of the legs was closer to 45 degrees than to 90 degrees; the accepted fifth position called for the heel of one foot to be placed by the metatarsals of the other foot, not toe-to-heel as it is today.

At the Paris Opera Ballet in the early 1950s, only two young ballerinas could achieve extensions close to 160 degrees; their arabesques left all gaping. Josette Amiel and Claude Bessy, brunette and blonde respectively, were often paired together in ballets in which their accomplishment could be highlighted by the choreographer.

This new-found ability to extend the legs at this dizzying height had a profound effect on ballet technique. Not only does it require more flexibility to execute extensions above 90 degrees, but it also requires more strength and cooperation from the muscles of the torso. Classroom exercises reflected this new thrust by emphasizing flexibility and extension. The entire line of the body became more extended. The strength that dancers developed through this emphasis led to the pyrotechnics of our age.

The wisdom of ballet's sequencing of exercises is now recognized by proponents of other techniques. Each technique addresses the need to stretch and strengthen, and each applies its concepts to center work in its own way. In a dance class every joint of the body should be gradually warmed, stretched, and strengthened. The structure of a modern-dance class follows a similar pattern: after the initial warmup exercises, balance, turns, jumps, and falls are practiced in combinations in the center and across the floor.

Ballet training has also come to be widely recognized and appreciated by dancers and choreographers as necessary for the development of a technical background. Ballet can be safely performed by the very young, and it most efficiently keeps a trained body in shape. Joe Orlando, a noted jazz teacher, gave this advice to a group of young students at a workshop: "If you can only do one class a day, make it a ballet class." The Alvin Ailey School, an enclave of modern dance, requires its summer students to take five ballet classes, two modern-dance classes and one jazz class a week, and at the Hubbard Street Dance Company, whose initial repertory was jazz, the company class is ballet.

· · ·

Before we move on to the next chapter, I would like to make a distinction between training methods and choreography. Training is the means by which a dancer arrives at a level of proficiency commensurate with her or his potential, and thereafter not only keeps in shape but has an opportunity to push the boundaries and achieve an ever subtler execution of motions. Choreography, on the other hand, is the use, usually by an individual but sometimes by a group working collaboratively, of a dance vocabulary to express an idea, tell a story, or explore the dynamics of motion. Most dance companies have a specific style within each discipline — ballet, modern, jazz, or tap. A company's style may be developed over a period of years and is usually guided by the vision of an individual, like the Royal Ballet in London under the leadership of Ninette de Valois, or the Joffrey Ballet with Robert Joffrey (1930–1989) or Gerald Arpino at the helm. The style may be narrow, like those developed at the New York City Ballet and the Martha Graham School, or it may be more inclusive, like that of the American Ballet Theatre, whose repertoire includes works by choreographers from Petipa to Twyla Tharp. Modern choreographers tend to develop individualistic styles that distinguish them from other choreographers, while ballet choreographers generally remain within the confines, more or less rigidly defined, of the ballet vocabulary.

Most dancers excel in one technique and concentrate their energies on that discipline in order to perfect it. Nevertheless, the study of ballet is central to improving technical proficiency for all dancers.

Students from the Academy of Movement
and Music in Oak Park, Illinois.
©1997 Mitchell Canoff

⚰ 2 ⚰

Dance Training

WHEN WE ENGAGE in any physical activity in a consistent manner over a period of time, we encourage the development of synaptic connections in the brain. These connections allow "new moves" to become part of our vocabulary of motion, just as crawling, walking, and running become part of our automatic response. These learned systems share a common feature: a broadening of the base of habitual actions that we can use consciously and with intent. When we talk of technique, we refer to training methods that employ a patterning process, that is, the repetition of specific motions until these motions become part of our physical vocabulary.

Basic motions are the building blocks of any technique and are usually selected because they support the style desired. Style can be understood as the result of choices made during training. For example, a person who has played golf for a long time is not necessarily good at tennis, because each sport employs specific actions that apply only peripherally to other sports. More often than not, style and technique are so intimately bound from the earliest stages of training that it is difficult to say where technique ends and style begins. Balinese dance, for example, has characteristic hand gestures and a rhythmic pattern that distinguishes it from African dance, in which the hand gestures are much freer in form and the rhythmic patterns are more dynamic. Both dance forms have specific and distinct methods of instruction.

Techniques build vocabulary by going from the simple to the complex. Basic motions are repeated over and over again, and eventually these motions can be linked into combinations. At first, combinations are limited to two or three basic motions; as the student progresses, the combinations become more complex, although they will still be comprised of the basic motions. When a method of teaching moves too quickly into the complex (a series of motions linked together) and overlooks the learning of basic motions in the very early stages of training, the building blocks, or steps of the technique, are not delineated in the student's mind and are therefore not clear in the execution of the motions.

I refer to "primary techniques" as those methods that teach basic motions over a long enough period of time to allow the synaptic connections in the brain to be formed. Another crucial component of dance training is the developed ability to maintain posture in some areas of the body while performing energetic actions with other parts of the body. This stabilization is essential to controlled movement. Both ballet and Graham techniques are based on this concept. A primary technique will also facilitate the learning of another technique. For example, a dancer who has integrated a primary technique learns other styles faster than one without training or with poor training. Theoretically, any technique can be primary if it develops specific motions as the basic building blocks of that particular dance form.

I advocate ballet as a primary technique for would-be dancers because it has developed definitive teaching tools, both in its choice of exercises and in their sequencing. In good ballet training (unfortunately, not all ballet teaching adheres to the principles of the art form), for at least the first two years, the students holds the arms in second position (to the side) while concentrating on the motions of the legs. Combining the movements of the arms and legs is very gradual. After focusing on leg motions, the student performs arm-movement sequences while standing in position, that is, in isolation from leg motions. Later on, the two elements will be performed together, but only after the path of the arms and the path of the legs have been established separately. In ballet, "isolation" consists of inhibiting certain responses; the student learns not to lift the shoulder when lifting the arm, or not to shift the pelvis when lifting a leg. Each exercise is performed in its most basic form until the integrity of the isolated motion has been established. The position of the arm and the posture of the body are especially critical, because conscious control of these body parts is crucial to the correct execution of all motions.

In our educational systems we have pitted creativity and formal elements of technique against one another. Some instructors seem to believe that the mere introduction of technique will compromise, if not kill, creativity. However, we need to remember that this arduous process is not an end in itself; it is only the means. It is the acquisition of tools that will allow the artist to freely utilize imagination and creativity. We learn technique to be able to forget it, transcend it, and communicate fully our intent. Creativity needs tools to help fashion ideas, to bring them into concreteness. Art begins with a conscious intent. Dance is a most intimate art because it uses the body in its creation. When we ignore the technical aspects of an art form, we deny ourselves the benefit of an established vocabulary that inevitably provides an underpinning for our originality.

The purpose of dance training is the acquisition of technique. One definition of technique is "a method of accomplishing a desired aim." The aim of dance instruction is to train the body into an expressive and responsive instrument. A violinmaker selects the wood, prepares it, shapes it, fashions the pieces together, polishes it, and, finally, attaches the strings. Only then is the instrument ready to be played. Early dance training can be compared to the building of a violin. Specific methods and tools facilitate the task within each stage. For example, the pieces will not be glued together before each one is the correct shape, nor the strings attached before the glue has set.

In dance, the building of the instrument is dependent on our physical and mental development. We must learn to walk before we can run. As we learn to walk, we develop habits that will serve the act of running more or less efficiently depending on the neuromuscular connections we have established. Although new scientific research is providing us information about various aspects of our being that were mysteries a century ago, the human body has not evolved at the same pace. We are still limited by a rate of growth both mental and physical.

No matter what teaching methods we use, we still cannot expect a two-year-old to grasp concepts of higher mathematics. If the aim of taking dance classes is the acquisition of skills, then the progression of training that I suggest in this book can be seen as a logical, developmental process designed to serve the purpose.

Initially, creative movement introduces children to non-formal dance. Ballet, modern dance, and tap can be studied concurrently to develop formal movement patterns, rhythmic and spatial awareness, and a creative approach to motion. Jazz is not a technique but a style. Jazz incorporates aspects of ballet, modern, African, and tap and modifies them stylistically into a dynamic dance form. Jazz may be compared to musical theatre, which incorporates dancing, singing, and acting but is not a discipline unto itself. A musical theatre artist needs to take dance, voice, and acting lessons to perfect skills in those areas before putting them all together and applying them to the musical theatre repertory.

What one chooses to do with the instrument one has built depends on individual taste, preference, and, ultimately, choreography.

THE EARLY YEARS: CREATIVE MOVEMENT AND PRE-BALLET

Creative movement and pre-ballet are both based on the idea of providing physical activity for children who are too young for formal technical training. (Before seven or eight, children's bones are too soft, their muscular connections insufficiently established, and their attention spans too short to focus on technical issues.) Generally, creative movement is taught by modern-dance teachers and pre-ballet by classically trained teachers, Some schools teach both, beginning with creative movement for the very young and then moving on to pre-ballet for a slightly more technical approach.

The activities devised to enhance movement awareness may be based on the Swiss music teacher Emile Jaques-Dalcroze's (1865–1950) system of movement. Although this system was developed to train young musicians, not dancers, to express rhythms through movement, it is a wonderful system for all children who need to develop coordination between what is seen or heard and a specific physical response.

Some modern dance methods also allow full participation by very young children when they do not stress formal motion. The child is free to express feelings and ideas with movement in a nonjudgmental environment. Improvisational techniques are also a good beginning for children, stressing group activity and an awareness of both space and other people.

Creative-movement classes generally place emphasis on shape, space, and response to different sounds or rhythms. The classes challenge the child's imagination, heightening awareness both of the body and how it moves through space and of relationships to others who share that space and create patterns. They achieve this goal through the use of musical games, storytelling in movement, and mimicry of our natural environment — clouds, rain, waves, flowers, trees, animals. They also sharpen perception of spatial relationships as well as shapes and dynamics. Through these activities and others — such as gentle stretching and gross motor-control motions, like skipping and marching — children learn to give physical expression to their visualizations, and to develop motor-control coordination.

The teacher of creative movement is typically responsive to and supportive of the shapes and motions the child creates, and encourages the discovery of new shapes or alternate ways of moving.

A pre-ballet class incorporates some of the elements of creative movement. It also introduces some basic classical-ballet positions and motions without emphasizing their technical aspects.

While both types of classes develop flexibility, coordination, and sensitivity to music and rhythm, children also discover the pleasure of kinetic self-expression within a framework that challenges their perceptions. Ideally, the structure of the class allows for enough freedom of expression to give children a sense that they are participating in a discovery, not that there are right or wrong responses to directions. This approach enhances the child's self-image and develops self-confidence along with physical and spatial skills.

BEGINNING FORMAL TRAINING: BALLET AND TAP

(Most dance studios do not include modern dance in their curriculum for ages seven to twelve).

Ballet enlarges, formalizes, and redirects the movement vocabulary that is naturally available to us — walking, running, twisting, bending, flaying the arms, kicking the legs, and shaking the head. Through the repetition of simple motions that increase in complexity as the technique is integrated, ballet builds a musculature that is both strong and flexible and increases the range of motion of the joints. It fosters a balanced alignment and good posture, and it allows children to develop at an early age the necessary coordination and movement skills that will enable them to respond and adapt to other movement styles. Ballet is a primary technique because it teaches a basic movement vocabulary and relies on the stabilization concept for the execution of that vocabulary. However, it should not be introduced to children before age seven at the earliest. Many schools offer tap classes for students in this age group. Tap promotes coordination, an acute sense of rhythmic patterns, and, above all, it is fun — an attribute not always found in ballet. In addition, like ballet, tap encourages the retention of movement patterns and thus aids in the development of kinetic memory (the ability to remember specific movements and sequences of movements).

In a ballet class, initial practice is limited to approximately five of the ten distinct exercises that are performed at the barre. As the body gets stronger, further exercises are introduced until all ten are known and practiced. Along with the exercises, the five positions of the feet and the arm positions are learned. Basic jumps are also introduced.

These exercises are basic because they involve basic movements that establish pathways for all later motions. Motions of the leg are stretching the straight leg, flexing the ankle or the knee, flexing the leg at the hip joint, moving the leg to the front, back, and side, and circular motion at the hip joint and at the knee. Motions of the arms are front, side, and overhead. Positions of the head are straight forward, tilted, turned, and circular. Similarly, the basic jumps develop the action that will be necessary for all jumps. (There are only four ways to jump: from two feet to two feet, from two feet to one foot, from one foot to two feet, and from one foot to one foot).

The traditional barre practice begins with plié, the bending of the knees and flexion at the hip and ankle joints in the five positions.

Young beginners practice only three of the five. There are two versions of the plié: demi (half) and grand (deep). Initially only the demi plié is practiced.

First position: feet turned-out to 45 degrees heel to heel.
Second position: feet apart, to the side, separated by about a foot and a half.
Third position: the heel of one foot placed in front of the other in a tight position.

Positions introduced later in the training process, when the musculature can cope with a greater degree of turn-out, are:

Fourth position: feet placed in front of one another in an open position, separated by about a foot.
Fifth position: feet placed heel-to-toe in front of one another.

The remaining exercises are:

Battement tendu (stretching): the leg is stretched out to front, side, or back, the toes pointing but never leaving the floor.

Battement tendu jeté (throwing motion) or degagé (disengagement, terminology of the Italian School): the leg is stretched out in the same way as in a battement tendu, but the toes come off the ground to a height of about 45 degrees.

Rond de jambe par terre (circular motion): with the toes never leaving the floor, the leg describes a circle from front to back and back to front, passing through first position.

Battement frappé (hitting or striking): a percussive motion from the knee down. The working leg's heel is placed on the ankle of the supporting leg, and the leg is then stretched out in a fast motion (initially to toes touching the floor, subsequently to a 45-degree angle off the floor) to the front, side, or back. Beginners master the side position first.

These exercises comprise the vocabulary for the first year of training. The other exercises are as follows:

Battement fondu (melting motion): begins with a a plié on the supporting leg while the other is placed in a retiré position (knee bent, toes touching the supporting leg in front or back). Proceeds to a full extension in the air while the supporting leg is straightened.

Rond de jambe en l'air (circle of the leg in the air): the leg is lifted to the side, eventually to 90 degrees off the floor, and the lower leg describes a small circle either outward or inward (outward is a motion from back to front, and inward is from front to back). The action is limited to the knee joint.

Developpé (enfolding): the working leg is lifted to a high extension, passing through a retiré position.

Petit battement sur le cou de pied (little beating on the ankle): the heel of the working foot is placed on the ankle of the supporting leg and strikes the ankle back and front. The action is limited to the knee joint.

Grand battement (big leg lifts): the working leg is lifted straight upward as high as it will go and returns to a closed position before the next battement.

The terminology for the positions of the arms varies greatly from school to school, but there are only two basic positions. In the first, the arms are down, slightly rounded, and held in front of the body; the same position can be lifted to a place just in front of the sternum, first position, and also above the head, fifth position. In the second position, the arms are held to the side just below shoulder height. All other positions are derived from these basic ones.

These exercises prepare both the musculature and the brain to perform all the potential movements of the vocabulary and to respond efficiently to directions. Moreover, the basic exercises lend themselves to manipulation; any number of variations on the theme can be devised to emphasize a concept or introduce a notion.

The ballet class continues with work in the center of the floor. Initially the vocabulary is limited to a handful of basic steps. Eventually the students will perform some exercises from the barre repeated in short sequences; these may include turns. They will then perform adagios (slow, sustained motions of legs in extensions) to test balance and coordination. Then come the jumps, first small jumps close to the floor, then big ones across the floor.

When building a house, one must establish a level and sound foundation to ensure the soundness of the rest of the structure. Ballet provides this foundation for dance. It does not exclude the introduction of modern-dance concepts, which many teachers are now providing after the basics have been integrated. Young dancers are engaged in enlarging their movement vocabulary and their awareness of movement potential. They are building a house in which they will live the rest of their lives.

TAP-DANCE TRAINING

Tap focuses on the sounds and rhythms that can be obtained through the control of dynamics and energy. The knees and ankle joints are relaxed enough to allow free motion of the feet. Initially children learn basic rhythms by using either the heel or the toe to produce the sounds. Eventually, more complex rhythms can be obtained with accompanying motions of the legs and body, which may include leaps and turns. Dexterity, quickness, and a relaxed stance are encouraged. Although some formal arm positions may accompany the tapping, they are open to a freer interpretation than ballet positions allow.

A tap class includes the practice of specific rhythmic patterns and may end in short routines, in which the material learned can be applied creatively.

MODERN DANCE TRAINING

It is much harder to categorize the training methods of modern dance because it has always been motivated by an individual need for self-

expression. Far more voices exist in modern dance than in ballet training, which precludes a universal measurability. For example, the
Humphrey-Weidman technique is spatially oriented, whereas the Graham technique is based on the experience of one's own center. Although a choreographer may devise original training-movement
sequences that lead logically to utility in choreography, there are some
features that are common to all styles. Some of these features are:

The concept of the center as the place where all movement originates,
as well as motions that are performed off-center.

The contraction, a hollowing inward of the abdominals until the spine
curves, and the release, which straightens the body out of the contraction. (There is no release of tension in the release.)

The use of the parallel positioning of the legs, and the study of how
this affects all extensions off the floor.

The use of the flexed foot.

An extensive use of prone movements.

The concept of fall and recovery as initiator of motion, and the study
of specific falls that illustrate this concept.

The attitude that questions any rule.

A modern-dance class may begin with exercises on the floor (Graham technique) or standing up. The standing exercises include motions already familiar from the ballet class but executed with the legs
both in parallel and turned-out positions, such as bending the knees in
a variety of positions (legs together and apart), often including a contraction and release; stretching the leg along the floor to full extension
(tendu); taking that motion off the floor (jeté); a variety of stretches of
the torso together with arm motions that can be either swinging or
sustained; and a variety of high leg extensions with tilts off-center and

contractions (adagio). This section of the class often ends with high kicks (grand battement). A variety of turns and leaps across the floor follow. Usually the teacher will choreograph a movement phrase to be learned and practiced.

The Conceptual method of modern dance introduces the dancer to formal elements of movement, such as shape, effort, and dynamics. This type of training can begin at an early age. However, when it does not practice basic formal motions, it fails to develop the necessary neuromuscular connections that are the basis of technique. Recent research confirms that children need formal kinetic training in order to develop these connections. As stated earlier, the repetition of simple physical motions that encourage synaptic connections in the brain are central to this development. Nevertheless, the Conceptual method encourages children to use their imagination and to discover movement patterns that are personally expressive.

Modern dance relies heavily on lineage. If a teacher advertises as a "Graham teacher," you can expect to learn the technique developed by Martha Graham. Merce Cunningham–trained teachers will be more balletic in their approach without, however, an emphasis on the classical line. Lester Horton (1906–1972) influenced a generation of dancers and teachers with a vigorous athletic style. Doris Humphrey developed a fluid style based on fall and recovery, giving in to the pull of gravity and resisting it in turn. José Limon, on the other hand, explored the circularity and connectedness of motion. These are a few of the innovators whose precepts have been accepted and are utilized to a greater or lesser degree by most contemporary modern dancers and teachers.

At the age of twelve to fourteen, the study of the Martha Graham technique can begin. This method demands a great deal of control and awareness. It relies on dynamics and concepts that require an intellectual as well as a physical response. This type of control and introspection are not available to younger children, and, therefore, it is better to wait until they are old enough to engage these skills and can draw full benefit from this technique.

Graham devised an extensive vocabulary of floor exercises which includes contraction, release, and spiraling of the torso with accompanying head, arm, and legs motions. These are rigorous movements and presume a measure of control of the spinal column and hip joint. The Graham class starts sitting on the floor to execute a series of formal exercises with emphasis on the torso's ability to contract, release, and spiral. The legs are stretched and bent and the instep flexed or pointed, depending on the exercise. The arm and head positions are an integral part of each motion. The next section of the class may include some of the standing exercises mentioned earlier. The class ends with turns and leaps across the studio. A Graham class is even more regimented than a ballet class, and true exponents of the technique do not waver from the structure or the content.

I want to emphasize that we are not discussing choreographic merits but presenting an overview of training methods. Many formally trained dancers have turned their backs on their primary technique and gone on to create original movement in their choreography. Their choreographic output cannot be confused with training methods.

As I mentioned earlier, modern dance and ballet have discovered that their techniques are not mutually exclusive. Ballet technique is valued by modern dancers for its ability to keep the body tuned. Although some modern movements, such as the deep contraction, have no counterpart in the balletic training vocabulary, they are often used choreographically in ballet. Both techniques require a strong sense of center, or knittedness. Isadora Duncan considered the center to be located at the solar plexus, the area around the sternum; she said that all movement comes from that center. *Center* refers to the general area of the belly, which is, in actuality, the body's center of gravity. An awareness of that part of the body is an essential aspect of all motion and is strongly emphasized in the modern technique. It helps to enhance the strength of the spine as well as access the deep muscles of the torso. Moreover, motions that involve prone positions on the floor have been freely adopted by contemporary ballet choreographers. Today's dancer should be versed in both techniques to be able to respond fully to choreographic demands.

JAZZ TRAINING

Many schools teach jazz to young children as a primary technique, borrowing the training vocabulary from ballet and modern. If the training method addresses a basic movement vocabulary as well as the stabilizing concept and does not overly stress the learning of routines, students may achieve technical proficiency. However, if learning routines predominates, students will not have the opportunity to develop solid technical knowledge.

As in modern dance, there are several jazz styles, ranging from the overtly sexual to the powerfully dynamic. The sensuality inherent in jazz movement is an adult expression, its movements having evolved on adult bodies whose spines and hip sockets are fully developed. Childrens' bodies, still in the process of growth, are not equipped to cope with the motions, often violent, that the style demands. Although in jazz the concept of isolation holds a central place, it does not seem to foster the kind of stability that ballet and Graham techniques encourage.

A degree of control needs to be established before jazz isolations can be executed safely. Mary Beth Kisner, director of the Conservatory of American Dance and artistic director of Chi-Town Jazz Dance, is emphatic about a progression of training that begins with ballet as the foundation. She says that she does not want to see students in her class before they are sixteen and have acquired a solid grounding in ballet technique.

Jazz classes rely heavily on the movement vocabulary of both ballet and modern dance in the formulation of their exercises. Most of the exercises we have already described are part of the jazz class, which may start with dancers standing at the barre or in the center depending on the preference of the teacher. The motions are usually more percussive than in either ballet or modern. The hands are often splayed, fingers strongly extended. The structure of the class is, again, similar to that in the other two techniques. After the warmup exercises, students learn shorter or longer combinations of motions, often called routines, which include turns and leaps.

The study of modern and ballet techniques enables the student to adapt quickly to the requirements of jazz, but the converse is seldom true. The student who starts dance training with jazz lessons has greater difficulties adapting to the requirements of the other two disciplines and sometimes cannot overcome the partiality of that early training. However, children enjoy the kinetic aspects of jazz and generally find the style more accessible than either ballet or modern. Nevertheless, the wise parent will keep the ice cream for the end of the meal, after the vegetables and protein have provided the nourishment necessary for the body's growth. Jazz studies should ideally begin after age fifteen, when the musculature and the brain patterns have had a chance to develop.

The ideal sequence of studies is:

AGE	CLASS
4–8	Creative movement, pre-ballet
7–14	Ballet, tap, modern
14–16	Ballet, tap, modern (Graham)
15–18	Ballet, tap, modern, jazz

This sequence is by no means a blueprint; the ages are approximate, and late starters can follow an accelerated course of studies. Additionally, after some basic technique has been acquired, the child may choose to devote more time to one form.

To summarize, a teacher should advocate a logical choice of dance disciplines depending on the student's age, as well as a logical progression through each discipline's curriculum. Before age seven or eight, a nontechnical approach will provide a good introduction to dance through creative movement or pre-ballet classes. At age seven or eight, ballet classes can begin to build the necessary physical foundation through the basic motions of the ballet vocabulary. At the same time, tap can provide an extra physical outlet as it sharpens coordination and rhythmic awareness. Additionally, study of Conceptual modern dance can continue to foster creativity and imagination. After age thirteen or fourteen, the young dancer can be introduced to the Graham technique, and after age fifteen, to jazz.

A word of caution: more is not always better. Many schools offer interdisciplinary classes: in one hour students will learn a bit of ballet, a bit of jazz, some tap, and maybe even gymnastics. The children will not be bored; they will be too busy changing shoes! Enough time should be devoted to one activity for students to develop basic awareness and coordination within a discipline; one hour of a specific technique a week will do more than a lot of activities combined. In skipping from one activity to another, the students lose the advantage of repeating the simple movement patterns that help them develop the capacity to respond to a wide range of movement possibilities, nor will they develop the ability to focus, which is an essential part of any learning process.

OTHER DISCIPLINES

Sports and gymnastics, although worthwhile activities in and of themselves, do not help a dancer develop a dance technique. The synapses formed in sports activities are not transferable to dance. However, a child with a natural kinetic intelligence and a sports or gymnastics background may adapt easily to dance requirements once the initial patterning of those disciplines has been modified. Similarly, lifting weights will make you stronger but will not help you to dance the tango.

STARTING DANCE AS AN ADULT

So far, I have described the schedule for a student who begins dance at an early age. However, even late beginners can develop good technique. The late teen years are not too late to begin dance training. Boys in particular, who often avoid taking dance classes because of peer pressure and the sexual stereotypes associated with male dancers, can achieve good results even with a late start. Many professional male ballet dancers did not start until they were in their late teens or even early twenties. Modern dance allows for a more individual line; many modern dancers started dance in their college years and went on to build stellar careers. Much depends on the physical endowment of the person and on his or her desire to dance.

Whether students begin at age seven, ten, twenty, or forty the progression in learning the technique is the same; the elements to be integrated are the same. If you are a late beginner, anywhere from fifteen years old to seventy, you will understand the movement intellectually faster than an eight-year-old would. Your kinetic response and your musculature, however, will still need to catch up with your understanding.

In my early thirties, I began studying modern dance. Arrogantly, I thought that I was a trained dancer and did not need to attend beginners' classes. I enrolled in an intermediate Graham class and was quickly humbled. The first month was sheer hell! I struggled to keep up in a class where the teacher would simply announce the exercise and everyone around me would immediately begin the sequence, while I trailed a beat behind in an attempt to duplicate what I was seeing. Had I gone to a beginners' class, all of these exercises would have been explained, and the process of integration would have been much faster and certainly more pleasant.

Dance is a demanding and complex skill requiring patience and determination for full mastery. All of the muscles are involved in any single motion, either supportively or actively, and coordinating these elements can be initially intimidating. The good news is that a beginners' class will cover the same basic material over a period of time, gradually building proficiency.

Ballet may be daunting because it strives for a particular line or shape. As proficiency grows, our perceptions of the motions change and demand an ever greater effort to achieve the ideal. The greatest benefit of ballet exercises comes from a correct execution of the motions. At the beginning, students strive to perform a motion without regard to form (e.g., straight knees or pointed toes). But as the motion becomes routine, the mind becomes free to address concerns of form, shape, and effort; students begin to truly enjoy the activity. To arrive at this point takes patience; integration of the basic elements may take a long time. The wonderful thing about ballet is that it lets students progress at their own pace, and it provides the opportunity to correct a variety of problems within the same exercise. For example, in a battement tendu exercise, one student may concentrate on stretching the knees while another works on extending the arch of the instep; someone else may be thinking about keeping the shoulders down with the arm in position. The corrections and directives of the teacher will indicate the areas that both the class and the individual need to address.

Because of modern dance's individualistic nature, taking a trial class with several different teachers may help you select the one that comes closest to what you expect from a dance class. Although greater freedom of interpretation is inherent in the modern technique, the motions practiced in class are usually as specific as those practiced in a ballet class; patience and perseverance are again needed in order to integrate the motions and gain the greatest benefit from the activity.

The enjoyment of dancing need not be limited to people who intend to become dancers. Adults, just as much as children, can benefit from the discipline. Most studios offer adult-beginner classes, and when you feel confident with the vocabulary, you can join any number of open classes in professional studios.

In one of my classes for adults, there was a woman who had taken lessons as a child. Ballet class for her was a means of recapturing the magic of her growing-up years. Twice a week, this insurance executive, dressed in her pink tights and little black skirt, became a ballerina again and twirled around with deep concentration and obvious enjoyment. Others came for the exercise and the opportunity to move to beautiful music. Although dance is not an aerobic activity, it brings all the muscles of the body into play, tones them up, and stretches them. Because dance emphasizes balanced alignment, it can help dissipate the stressful activities of the day that create areas of tension in our bodies. Most importantly, it creates a quiet zone for the psyche; for an hour-and-a-half the outside world recedes, leaving us only the motion and the music.

There is no age limit on performing. Many cities have an elder-citizen dance group that performs at nursing homes and hospitals. One of my dance friends was honored by being asked to join such a group in Great Fall, Montana. At thirty, she was the youngest member in the group, whose ages ranged from fifty to seventy. On one memorable occasion, when she was returning from a trip, she was met at the airport by the entire group in full costume. They proceeded to regale her and other passengers to a tap dance from their repertory.

Students from the Academy of Movement
and Music in Oak Park, Illinois.
©1997 Mitchell Canoff

⚓ 3 ⚓

How to Select a Teacher and School

I N THE PROCESS of choosing a school or a teacher, you should bear in mind two ideas: (1) This is not a life decision; (2) This may be a life decision. The first will help you avoid the sense of competition and urgency that often leads to unwise decisions, such as pressuring the child to excel beyond the capacity of her or his age, or choosing a school or teacher for the wrong reasons (it has the biggest enrollment in the area, or it puts on the most lavish recital at the end of the year). The second will guide you to choose wisely a teacher who can instill a sound foundation that will serve your dancer throughout her or his career.

Like most dancers and dance teachers, I am often asked how I started dancing. Initially, there was no thought of my becoming a professional; my mother simply decided that I needed to take ballet classes to conquer my shyness, straighten my legs, and relax my shoulders enough to show that I had a neck.

Among our acquaintances was Vala, a Russian emigré who had been a dancer. When my mother decided that I should dance, she asked Vala to suggest a teacher, and I was taken to Olga Preobrajenskaya (1870–1962). I was lucky; Preo was one of the most admired teachers of that time. She had been a prima ballerina at Russia's Maryinski Theater, and she imparted to her students the great tradition of classicism as she had experienced it on the Imperial stages and in the studios of Marius Petipa, Christian Johansson, and Enrico Cecchetti. But her greatest recommendation was that she was a wonderful teacher — clear in her presentation, demanding without being over-bearing, and stylistically immaculate.

I think my introduction to dance was fairly typical; most children begin ballet classes because their parents believe ballet is an activity that will benefit the child. Eventually, the child's interest may surpass that of the parent, and a dancer in the making is born!

. . .

In America's early colonial days and through the nineteenth century, French and Italian dancers performed in our major cities. Some were hired to teach dance and deportment to young ladies of good families; some settled here and taught privately. But ballet did not flourish in American culture until the beginning of the twentieth century. At this time, Russian dancers, such as Anna Pavlova, toured the country and introduced the Russian style to bemused audiences. Additionally, many major cities supported opera houses with resident ballet com-panies. The Russian Revolution brought the greatest influx of Russian dancers and teachers to these shores.

The Revolution also forced Diaghilev's Ballets Russes to remain in the West. After Diaghilev's death in 1929, the company performed under the names of Ballets Russes de Monte Carlo and Ballets Russes du Colonel de Basil. By that time, most of the original dancers had left the stage and were teaching in Europe and the United States. The style taught today in America owes much to these early emigrés, including Mikhail Fokine, Adolph Bolm (1884–1951), Michael Mordkin (1880–1944), Piotr Vladimiroff (1893–1970), and Anatole Oboukhoff (1896–1962). When teachers say they are following a Russian method, they usually mean that they have studied with one of these masters or with one of these masters' former students.

The conditions of teaching in America were very different from the ones that saw the flowering of the Russian ballet, a system mod-eled on the French ballet and used to this day. In the Russian system, ten-year-old children are selected for the State school on the basis of their physical attributes. For eight years, they receive academic as well as dance and music education, undergoing a process of selection every year. Those who make it through to the end are guaranteed work either in the city where they studied or some other location. Even large companies, like the Kirov or the Bolshoi, cannot guarantee a place for all graduating students. Occasionally, an outstanding dancer from the provincial cities, like Mikhail Baryshnikov (b.1948), who began his studies in Riga, is transferred to the most prestigious Kirov.

When the ties with Mother Russia were broken, most emigré dancers began teaching in open studios, meaning that they employed an ungraded system. Classes were generally at an intermediate-to-advanced level, and anyone could take them. In the 1930s, some teachers began to offer a more systematic approach to dance education, notably Catherine Littlefield (1905–1951) in Philadelphia, George Balanchine (under the auspices of Lincoln Kirstein, 1907–1997) in New York's School of American Ballet, and Marie Rambert (1888–1982) and Ninette de Valois in England.

An open studio generally offers classes on a per-class basis. Although their instruction may be excellent, these studios are best suited to advanced and professional dancers, because they cannot follow a developmental curriculum due to their largely transient student body. However, most dancers studying in the early twentieth century were educated in this fashion.

Today, in the major cities, many studios offer ungraded classes throughout the day, and a graded program for children as well as classes for adults in the late afternoon and evening. In smaller towns, where there is no group of professional dancers, studios generally offer classes for children and adults after school hours. Additionally, many established ballet companies have an associated school, such as the New York City Ballet's School of American Ballet, the San Francisco Ballet and School, the Pacific Northwest Ballet School in Seattle, the Houston Ballet and School, the National Ballet School in Toronto, and the Royal Winnipeg Ballet School, to name a few.

SELECTING A SCHOOL

In metropolitan areas, the choices of dance schools are numerous, which paradoxically makes the search for a teacher more difficult. Selecting a school should not be a casual matter. Opting for the convenience of a studio close to home should be weighed against the reputation of the school. Even personal recommendations from other parents need to be investigated. A visit to the school and a talk with the teacher are certainly in order. Observe a few classes (not only the one your child will attend, but also a couple of other levels to ascertain the progress of the students) and make a note of the teacher's relationship to the students and the tone maintained in class.

This initial effort is important for one overriding reason: when you have chosen a school, you must be prepared to make a commitment, because changing schools may be detrimental to the progress of the child. To quote Ms. Kisner (Director of Chi-Town Jazz Company) again, "Dance in America is very disjointed. Everyone is skipping from teacher to teacher. I'm seriously concerned. I see the confusion in the eyes of the students." Learning to dance is similar to learning any other skill: it requires consistency to provide enough time for the skill to be assimilated and to become second nature. Although all ballet teachers presumably teach ballet technique, some stylistic differences are common. For a pirouette, Teacher A may favor a preparation in fourth position with both legs in plié (bent knees), while Teacher B likes the back leg to be straight. A child who takes classes that advocate contrasting styles does not have the chance to assimilate either method, and will not be able to improve the performance of these turns because of the confusing messages transmitted to the muscles.

Types of Dance Schools

Professional Schools. Usually a child is placed in a professional school after several years of preliminary training. Some professional schools, however, offer programs for young, beginning students. For older students, entrance into a professional school is generally by audition.

Some schools have a two-track program: the more serious students interested in a dance career follow one track, while the students who are attending mainly for recreation follow another. The Hartford School of Ballet in Hartford, Connecticut, is one school that offers this kind of program as well as teacher training in the Vaganova System. Some schools will not accept students with previous training older than fourteen (the School of American Ballet) or sixteen (The Joffrey School). However, their summer schools accept older students. These schools routinely recruit talented students and are usually able to offer substantial scholarships.

Professional schools, because of their affiliation with companies, generally subscribe to a particular style and employ teachers who have been trained in that style: Vaganova's style at the Hartford School; the English style at the Houston School; Balanchine's style at the School of American Ballet.

One of the many advantages of attending a professional school is the opportunity to take part in the productions of the sister company, such as the annual *Nutcracker*. Unlike the performances presented by private studios, where the students are the main performers, these productions place children within a greater whole. They allow them to learn the manners of the stage by watching professionals, who exemplify the standards that the children are striving for.

However, the competition at these schools is often fierce, and the demands for a high standard unbending. The individual personalities and needs of the students become secondary to their technical achievements; and while the students develop their technical skills, other aspects of their growth may be badly overlooked. Suzanne Gordon, in her book *Off Balance: The Real World of Ballet* (New York: Pantheon Books, 1983), writes about the overwhelming schedule at the School of American Ballet:

> Student dancers, like professionals, study six days a week. As they advance, they must do schoolwork, as well as take two or three classes a day. At the most advanced levels, they often dance in company productions; added to their normal course work are rehearsals and performances. This leaves little time for socializing. . . . In the world of ballet, dancers are often discouraged from engaging in any activity that might draw their attention away from dance.

This conditioning insulates the dancer from the outside world and predisposes the individual to adopt a tunnel vision in later life. Gordon quotes a dancer she interviewed: "You get out of touch with the world," says the San Francisco Ballet's Elizabeth Tienken. "You come home and you're tired and you don't want to listen to the news. I think we should all know what's going on in the world, but a lot of us don't, a lot of us block it out. We don't get involved, we don't vote. We say, oh, I don't need to know, I'm a dancer." Suzanne Gordon concludes: "Generally regarded as the tools of the choreographer, dancers are taught not to participate in the creative process. . . . Taught to obey orders rather than to think for themselves and encouraged to avoid the outside world, which is either a temptation or a trap, dancers begin to live in a cocoon."

While the top professional schools are the training ground for some outstanding performers, they tend to instill an all-or-nothing attitude in their students that precludes an objective assessment of the options open to dancers. Gordon quotes a student who gave up dancing at eighteen: "I was in New York, so I looked down on regional companies. I could have danced outside New York. I would have enjoyed dancing or teaching children," she says with sorrow, because she could not, when she was young, conceive of other options. "I only wish there was someplace else that kids could get that sense of dance."

The lure of New York and San Francisco is very strong for many dancers intent on a career; they perceive these two coastal cities as the apex of the profession. Yet the level of instruction in America today offers alternatives without compromise. Many dancers in New York received their initial training elsewhere; their competence attests to the standards set by their hometown schools and cannot be underestimated. Additionally, every major city is graced today by a ballet company; you need only to look at the listings in *Dance* Magazine to realize the extent of the choices dancers have for a fulfilling professional career.

Dance Programs in Public Schools. In the past twenty years, the value of arts has received wide recognition. While music, visual arts, and, in some instances, theatre have been an integral part of the education of our children for a long time, dance is a relative latecomer on the scene. In the 1980s, a strong thrust to establish dance education in public schools created dance programs in many states. However, not all programs are equal. Michelle Mathesius, chairperson of the dance department at La Guardia High School of Music and the Performing Arts, warns that a distinction must be made between enrichment programs and dance education:

The dance education I refer to focuses on sequential and highly specialized training leading to a professional career — serious dance education as distinguished from what might be termed "enrichment programs." I have nothing against enrichment programs as long as they make no false promises to those they serve. Unfortunately, many of today's programs fall into the enrichment category while implicitly promising that which can be delivered only through dance education. (*Joperd*, February 1992)

Mathesius succinctly outlines the elements that distinguish dance education from an enrichment program.

1. There must be a large pool of candidates from which to recruit. . . . There must be a rigorous audition process that all but guarantees the selection of highly motivated and extremely talented young dancers.

2. The faculty must be composed of artist/teachers — those that have dance expertise as a result of their dance performance experience.

3. Technique classes, the nuts and bolts of dance education, should be held sacred. Technical mastery is an essential goal and must be carefully taught with a regimen of daily classes in classical ballet and modern dance.

4. Live music is a vital component of every dance class. Any serious institute which trains dancers for the profession, without exception, provides each technique class with a musician.

5. A syllabus must be followed for technique classes that reflects demanding requirements and standards at all levels."

A number of states offer dance as part of arts education through their magnet programs (see appendix for listings). While the majority of these schools are high schools, a few elementary schools also specialize in the arts.

Typically, dance programs at magnet schools follow the model of a conservatory and are staffed by teachers who were professional dancers. Two to three hours of the school day are devoted to dance, a schedule that allows at least one technique class a day. The programs accept students through an audition process and offer ballet, modern dance, jazz, and sometimes tap. They may offer additional classes in dance history, kinesiology, or composition. Some, like Los Angeles County High School for the Arts, have classes in gymnastics, mime, and ethnic dance.

Some states have centers for the arts to which the students are bused throughout the day to attend specialized classes. One such program is located in Montgomery, Alabama, where the Carver Creative and Performing Arts Center has three sessions daily to provide training to different levels. Of a six-hour day, students devote two hours to dance training, which includes ballet, modern dance, and jazz.

Some school districts have Artist-in-Residence programs, through which an individual or a company may spend from one week to a full year at the school, working with the students. In a few instances, through the efforts of individual teachers, a dance program has grown from an extracurricular activity to a recognized entity within the broader curriculum of the school.

Ms. Mathesius's warning should be heeded. The early years of training are critical in a dancer's career; children who show both interest and promise need a program with the technical training that will allow them to fulfill their potential.

Private High Schools. Five private schools in the United States specialize in arts education: the Interlochen Arts Academy, in Michigan; the Walnut Hill School for the Arts, in Massachusetts; the Idyllwild School of Music and the Arts and the Crossroads School, both in California; and the Chicago Academy for the Arts. These schools offer a comprehensive arts and academic education (although the Crossroads School does not offer dance among its specialized majors). The students specialize in their chosen art form, but admission is granted through an audition process that tests both academic and artistic skills.

The advantages of attending these schools are numerous. They combine the benefits of a high school, where students receive their general education, with a studio program in the arts that is otherwise only available through a private studio. These schools typically offer a broad spectrum of dance-technique classes, taught by professionals, and supplementary subjects generally not taught in private studios, such as dance history, kinesiology, and composition; and of course they provide performing experience. They prepare the students for professional careers and for furthering their arts educations in university programs.

But perhaps the greatest contribution of these schools is the environment they provide, in which the students can grow as artists among kindred souls, within a community that appreciates and caters to this special group. There is no need to sacrifice social life, which is too often the price paid by dancers who attend dance classes after school.

For many dancers, a private high school for the arts offers a solution to the problem of obtaining a broad education without compromise.

Private Studio. Most dancers begin by taking classes at a private studio. Only when their interest and talent are assured will they seek a professional school or an arts high school to further their studies. Private dance schools, or studios, can offer a wide variety of programs. They are usually privately owned, and may range in size from one room in a residence to entire buildings comprised of numerous studio spaces.

A studio is usually administered by the principal teacher, who makes all decisions pertaining to its operation, including the hiring of other teachers. Many studios find it necessary for tax purposes to apply for nonprofit status, in which case a board of directors is selected. More often than not, the teacher will retain control by being president of the board.

These studios may specialize in ballet and offer tap and jazz classes; a few include modern dance in their curricula. A potential student can determine the emphasis a studio places on any one discipline by looking at its schedule of classes; more classes will be offered in the studio's favored technique.

Even relatively small private studios may have a performing group to provide an artistic outlet for their older students. These groups typically perform at social functions, in hospitals, or at local schools. Additionally, many private studios join organizations, such as the Dance Masters of America or The National Association of Dance Artists, which provide a forum for local teachers and an opportunity for students to take classes with a variety of teachers in ballet, tap, jazz, and modern.

Most schools form their classes by age group and level of proficiency. This grading takes into consideration the physical development of the children and the number of years they have been dancing, and may thus span two or three years. For example, a class may include a nine-year-old who has been dancing for three years and an eleven-year-old who has only one year of experience. Some schools follow a syllabus, like the Vaganova system, the Cecchetti method, or the Royal Academy of Dancing (the method developed in England in the 1930s that formed the basis of British ballet). More often than not, the principal teacher or director follows the training method that she or he studied, or with which she or he was professionally associated. For example, a teacher who was a member of the New York City Ballet will probably subscribe to the ideas advanced by George Balanchine and hire teachers who share that approach, thus creating a homogeneous base for all instruction carried out at the school.

Unless the school specifies its affiliation by declaring that it teaches a specific method, it can be assumed that the technique taught is a good old American hybrid. The melting pot is alive and well in the dance field and has produced some outstanding performers as well as pedagogues.

In large cities, some schools operate on the model of the open studio. They offer ungraded classes that students can attend without having to enroll for a full semester. These classes are usually at an intermediate or advanced level, and are therefore beneficial to dancers who have reached a level of proficiency that allows them to take full advantage of the material covered in the class.

ABOUT TEACHERS

Although, thanks to college programs in dance, dancers today are as likely as other professionals to have a degree, there are still many dance teachers who bypassed this qualification because of their professional commitments.

Modern dancers are more likely than ballet dancers to have a college degree. They often start dancing at a later age, in college, and tend to be more cerebral in their approaches to dance. This allows them to weigh teaching methods and to be more impartial in their approach.

In contrast, the traditional path for a ballet dancer takes the student from a pre-professional school, through the ranks of the corps de ballet, to a position as a soloist in a company. However, in today's competitive world, dancers realize the need for education, and many pursue degrees and a professional career at the same time. After a professional performing career, the dancer sometimes turns to teaching.

In reality, the simplicity of this progression is seldom experienced. Through the thirty-odd years that encompass both the training period and the professional career, a dancer may study with a variety of teachers in different schools and join various companies, as the need to work with a certain choreographer or the dissatisfaction with a particular repertoire dictates. The better qualified, more adaptable dancer will find greater opportunities.

Dancers are gypsies. They go where work is available, stay as long as they are challenged and appreciated, and move on, either because they have been offered better contracts or because their present contracts have not been renewed. Eventually they may return to their hometowns and open up schools. Many adopt new cities and stay on to teach at the school of the company in which they performed.

Economic realities play a large role in determining when a dancer begins to teach. Many dancers are freelance artists, dancing a season with one group, then a season with another, often with periods of no engagements in-between. To supplement their incomes, they may teach. However, schools that rely on professionally active dancers to make up their faculty may inadvertently do a disservice to their student body by failing to provide continuity in the training. This consideration is especially true for the beginning levels, when consistency is very important.

At the turn of the century, renowned ballet master Enrico Cecchetti wrote an open letter to his students in Russia cautioning them to choose teachers who had completed their performing careers. The reason for this injunction is still valid today: dancers are in training throughout their performing careers, necessarily focusing on personal solutions to the challenges of their technique. After they have stopped dancing, dancers may find the leisure to reflect on the technique as a whole and to begin to recognize how it affects body types that are different from their own. This sentiment is echoed by Karel Shook in the introduction to his book, *Elements of Classical Ballet Technique* (1977).

Talking specifically about young teachers, he says: "The mistaken idea that the elementary grades in dance instruction, regardless of the beginner's age, can be taught with any success in the absence of strict supervision, by neophyte teachers or advanced students, has to be discarded immediately. These elementary levels are the most difficult and demanding to teach."

Language gives us a further clue to the transition that every dancer must make to become a teacher — we say a dancer "takes" class, whereas a teacher "gives" class. Thus teachers refocus their attention to become fully responsive to the needs of their students. In guiding them through the technique, teachers offer their knowledge as a gift to their students, who take the gift and further fashion it to meet their individual requirements. Some people make the transition from dancer to teacher more gracefully than others, and they are the ones who make the better teachers. Furthermore, the level of proficiency or recognition a teacher achieved during his or her career does not guarantee greater effectiveness as a teacher. A prima ballerina is not necessarily a better teacher than someone who has only been in the corps de ballet.

The teacher you select will probably have a list of professional credentials that establish her or his lineage and competence and indicate the type of technique to be taught. She or he may also have a college degree in dance or be certified to teach by the state, if employed in the public school system. A parent should feel free to ask for teachers' credentials and discuss with teachers the focus or approach that guides them. Coupled with observation of a class or two, interviews will provide a basis for determining good style and making a selection. The school brochure may provide some information, but asking questions may still be necessary.

Children initially learn by imitating their teachers, so it is important that teachers exhibit a clean body line free of mannerisms. All dancers develop idiosyncrasies, individual ways of performing motions that, when they do not interfere with the clarity of the gesture, can enhance and deepen expressiveness. However, when dancers become teachers, they must shed these mannerisms in order to transmit a pure line to their students. The ways teachers hold themselves, demonstrate the movements, and offer correction give testimony to the training they received; as with antiques, provenance is of utmost importance. Lastly, teachers should be able to explain the meanings of the French names used in the class and to fully engage the attention of their pupils. (To some extent, the French terminology is used by all techniques.)

Some teachers routinely attend summer workshops. These typically one- to two-week sessions are good forums for exchanging ideas as well as honing skills (particularly for young teachers), but they cannot replace a good early education and professional experience in the field. It takes years to integrate a technique, and while new concepts learned at summer workshops can serve to clarify teachers' ideas, they should not be used as a claim that the teacher is proficient in the method.

The ideal teacher should possess the following:

1. Credentials from a recognized institution: a professional school, company, or college

2. Some professional experience

3. A patient but not pampering attitude

4. Comfort with the material, and an ability to organize the material logically and appropriately for each age group

5. An ability to inspire a feeling of purpose and excitement among the students

6. A critical eye for making appropriate criticism in an encouraging manner

7. An ability to maintain concentration and discipline at all times

8. Above all, a love for the experience of dance, and an unselfish desire to see the students improve.

The Teacher's Role

The interaction between teacher and student is probably one of the most important aspects of the learning process; teachers must not only be knowledgeable, but must also possess a generosity of spirit that enables them to share their knowledge. One of the most unhappy periods of my training was two years spent with a teacher who routinely denigrated our intelligence and humiliated us. As punishment for our stupidity, she would send her current victim out of the studio to sit out the rest of the class. After trying to comply and do the exercises correctly, I eventually gave up and even devised ruses to avoid class. But this teacher was too perceptive to be fooled by a twelve-year-old. She would watch me make mistakes and would simply smile and turn away. Whatever the reasons may have been, her attitude denied us the joy of the dance and undermined our self-confidence as well as our will to work hard.

Dancers often suffer from low self-esteem. We tend to be overly critical and demanding of our performance and to accept compliments with strong reservations. Teachers who establish their authority through fear and humiliation feed this insecurity and damage both the individual and the dance. Although maintaining discipline in the studio is essential to good learning, other methods are available besides intimidation. By engaging the interest of the student, the teacher can diminish the need to enforce silence. Within a couple of years of study, students realize that they do not want to be distracted, that they need to direct all of their concentration toward the execution of the movement; and they derive pleasure from mastering the task.

In addition to the overtly physical training that takes place in class, another type of learning is taking place. Class time can serve as a time of meditation. We can retire from the everyday world to concentrate deeply on our own ability, looking toward the strength within that is the source of discipline. We admire artists for their ability to give themselves to the moment of creation, and we are told that in each of us there is an artist crying to be heard. Dance class provides that access; the teacher, like the Zen master, sets the tone and the example and leads students on a journey of self-discovery.

STRUCTURE OF STUDIES

A good school will provide continuity in instruction; in other words, it will have scheduled, progressive, or graded classes conducted by the same teacher throughout the year. Students need to become familiar with a teacher's style of presentation and pace. Only then can they begin to concentrate on the concepts that are presented, and only then can their progress be gauged. Any one lesson will be entirely devoted to a specific discipline, either ballet, tap, modern, or jazz. Your child will be placed at the appropriate level, and the teacher will suggest additional classes for the student to attend as she or he progresses through the curriculum. In the case of beginners who only take one class a week, the full hour is absolutely necessary in order to instill the principles of technique. After the student begins to take two or more classes a week, the necessity for the full class time to be devoted to one discipline is even more important. By that time, the student will know more vocabulary and will need to practice it. Class time should normally increase to an hour-and-a-quarter and then an-hour-and-a-half, which is the traditional length of a lesson. Once pointe work is introduced, the class may stretch to two hours.

THE TALENTED CHILD

The talented child will always attract attention and receive special encouragement from instructors. Beware, however, of the teacher/director who inappropriately pushes the child through the curriculum too quickly. Children with greater natural facility will execute the technique easily and with more accuracy than those less gifted. They may give the impression that they are ready, both emotionally and physically, to go on to the next level. Young musculature, however, requires time to develop to support the dance movements fully. Skipping through levels will leave big gaps in a child's integration and understanding of the technique and may ultimately result in areas of physical stress that are very difficult to correct. Hurrying the process is both unwise and unnecessary. If the musculature is not adequately prepared, the child will strain to achieve the positions demanded and will develop bad habits, such as areas of compensation — using the wrong muscles to produce a motion. In the end, the young dancer will have built an unresponsive musculature that may well overshadow natural talent.

The parent of the talented child needs to be alert to the motivation of teachers who push a child too fast. Are these teachers promoting the best interest of the child, or their own reputations? There are all sorts of would-be Svengalis among both teachers who establish a guru-like relationship with their students and people on the periphery who claim that they can introduce you to the "right" people to advance your child's career. Ultimately, only the talent of the dancer is needed for promotion. The most brilliant teacher cannot make a dancer from an unwilling or unsuitable body or soul. In fact, teachers do not "make" dancers at all; a good teacher will lead the student through an ever deeper understanding of the technique to the realization of her or his potential. The credit belongs to the student. Teachers may take pride that they have given the correct information, and may rejoice in the achievements of their pupils.

· · ·

To summarize, the type of school you select will depend upon the age and the needs of your child. Even if your public school offers a dance program, you may want to enroll your child in a private-studio program for a more focused training. If your initial choice of a school was a good one, there should be no need to switch. A serious studio will usually offer a program that leads students from the beginning to a pre-professional level. You may, however, want to consider enrolling your child in a private arts high school if she or he demonstrates a keen interest and shows promise.

Even the smallest cities offer some choice of instruction. In larger cities, the school associated with a ballet company will provide more intense instruction; however, independent studios can be equally demanding.

Even if you are quite sure that your child has no intention of becoming a professional dancer and is simply looking for a good activity, it is advisable to choose a reputable school for early training. If children study at a school that honors the traditional principles of ballet technique, they will experience something real, something of lasting value that will give them a deep appreciation of the art form and will enrich their lives forever. Similarly, if you are lucky enough to live in an area that offers creative modern dance for children, the experience of the discovery of movement, the ability to develop self-expression, and the broadening of the base of spatial perceptions will enhance your child's intellectual, physical, and emotional growth.

Students from the Academy of Movement
and Music in Oak Park, Illinois.
©1997 Mitchell Canoff

⚴ 4 ⚶

Progression of Training

THE TENDENCY in this country is to program a child's day with a variety of activities that leave little time for leisure and play. Admittedly, parents struggle with balancing careers and family and generally want to make sure that their children are engaged in worthwhile activities. I recently received a telephone inquiry about dance classes for a five-year-old. When I told the mother that this pre-ballet class met on Tuesdays, she answered, "I will have to see if I can reschedule my daughter's tennis lesson." The task of rescheduling was daunting because the child also studied piano, took swimming lessons, and participated in an acting workshop.

Something has been lost in this process of filling the day with named endeavors. The happiest memories from my childhood all stem from the hours I spent either alone or with friends playing unstructured games, inventing stories to act out or dance, building ships out of chairs, dressing in my mother's clothes, or, because it was a safer world then, taking the long way home from school to explore different parts of the city. We did not have television to interfere with our creative urges, shape our perceptions, and keep us rooted as spectators instead of participants. However, this overscheduling has another side effect: we are creating a nation of dabblers, people who invest a minimum of effort in their work, want the maximum return, and, when gratification is not instant, move on to the next thing.

In dance, as in other art forms, or indeed in any activity, a sincere commitment to the task is the first necessity. Learning to dance is a long-term commitment, because the rewards are not immediately evident. It is essential for parents to appreciate this process.

Every year, a number of new students at my school decide that they do not like to dance after a couple of lessons. More often than not, the parents tell me about the problem before allowing the child to give up. Because, in such cases, tuition is not refundable, many parents continue to bring the child to class for the remainder of the semester. The majority of these children begin to enjoy class after a few more weeks of practice and insist on continuing after the first semester is over.

Learning to enjoy the process is an integral part of learning to dance. The process consists of little steps, small triumphs, small challenges, some disappointments that may lead to new understanding, aching muscles, and blistered feet. Each level of ballet includes movements that illustrate a particular usage of the body and develop the musculature while enlarging the student's range and vocabulary of motion. Students' progress is not based on the number of new steps learned but rather on the gradual improvement in execution. It takes a long time to become a dancer — a minimum of ten years before a solid intermediate level is reached. Thus, it is important to honor the process and praise the child at each level of development.

DEVELOPING GOOD POSTURE

Certain features of ballet technique are stressed from the beginning of training and continue to be perfected throughout a dancer's life. Foremost among these features is good posture. This task involves the awareness that the supporting side is active although it does not move. The primary goal of early training is to achieve a balanced and aligned stance. Standing correctly aligned on two legs with the ability to transfer your body weight to one leg without losing this alignment are prerequisites for all motion. Thus the pelvis does not move when a leg is lifted off the floor. (In initial training, the legs do not rise above 45 degrees; later in training, with higher extension, the pelvis participates in the motion.) The shoulder does not rise when an arm is lifted into position. This ability is developed through the execution of a few exercises that foster strength in all the weight-bearing joints (hip, knee, ankle) as well as engage the muscles of the torso to strengthen the spine. Of course, all motions are performed with a degree of turnout and with the arms held in a rounded manner.

The ability to maintain a balanced stance depends upon the child's physical development. The development of the musculature proceeds at its own pace; some children are naturally more coordinated and kinetically aware than others and can thus reproduce the movement they see with more accuracy. Starting ballet classes before age seven will not necessarily produce a prodigy. On the contrary, it prolongs this initial stage of training and often results in the child deciding to stop lessons just at the time when she or he would be moving into a more exciting phase.

Correct posture is achieved through the practice of the basic vocabulary. These steps are the building blocks of all future motions; within them they encompass all the permutations of the ballet technique. As I mentioned earlier, these simple exercises create new synaptic connections that will allow the body to respond immediately to commands from the brain. In his seminal work on child development, Jean Piaget (1896–1980) identified the period from birth to age seven as the pre-operational stage. At this stage, thought and action have not yet developed the relationship that as adults we take for granted: we can externalize (manifest) our thought directly into action. Young children will often have trouble guiding their actions, because they have not yet developed a direct link between thought and action. This inability, coupled with a short attention span, severely curtails the kinds of physical activities that children can successfully participate in before age seven. The first two or three years of dance training are as basic to the development of the ballet technique as learning to crawl is to the child, and they carry the same implications: the motions learned become part of the innate vocabulary.

There was a woman who lived down the street from me in London who had a congenital hip defect that made her walk with a pronounced limp. Her three children also walked with a limp, even though they had not inherited the hip defect; they had simply learned to walk by imitating their mother.

Once the body is "placed" and the student has a basic grasp of the fundamental motions, she or he is ready to learn more of the steps of the technique, and class becomes more varied. There are only about fifty-six steps in the classical technique, but the ways in which they can be combined are endless. Progression through the technique consists of improving the execution of the motions as well as building stamina. It is not until a high-intermediate level has been reached that certain steps of the technique can be practiced; therefore, the vocabulary of motions is quite limited for the first six or seven years of training. The stretch of the instep, the line of the leg, the fluidity of the arms, secure balance, and smoothness of transitions are some of the markers that indicate progress in integrating the technique. These elements remain the primary concern of dancers throughout their life.

POINTE WORK

Generally, after about four years of study, the female student is ready to begin pointe work. The classroom preparation for this full rise onto the toes consists of exercises performed on half-pointe that strengthen the foot and familiarize the body with balancing on a smaller surface than the whole foot provides. Additionally, through preliminary regular classes, the student will have developed a strong back and a degree of control through the torso and the hip joint that allow her to maintain proper alignment.

It must be emphasized that the technique of dancing on pointe is not different from the technique required to perform the rest of the ballet vocabulary. The strength of the spine, hip, knee, and ankle joints is essential for the execution of all dance movements. Good alignment and a well-developed instep facilitate dancing both on pointe and off pointe. However, the extra effort required to rise on pointe and the ability to maintain a controlled light stance must be well developed before pointe work is introduced.

Not all feet develop the required curvature for dancing on pointe. Children with insufficiently arched feet will find going on pointe difficult regardless of their proficiency in other areas. Similarly, those with very high arches will have problems because their ankles and insteps will not offer sufficient support. In both cases, practice helps both to develop the arch further and strengthen the ankle joint.

Initially, ten to fifteen minutes is sufficient time to practice pointe work after the regular technique class. For the more advanced students, most schools schedule a full class on pointe once or twice a week. However, it will take a couple of years from the time the child first goes on pointe until the time she exhibits an adequate knowledge of the vocabulary and is physically able to cope with a full class on pointe.

The question of when to put a child on pointe has always stirred controversy. Some teachers have their students on pointe as early as age nine (which, in my opinion, is too early); others wait until the child is twelve. Establishing a desirable age between these two extremes is difficult because so much depends on the child's physical development and her ability to maintain the correct alignment. But to err on the side of conservatism is better than to cripple a young girl. The bones of the foot are among the last to ossify; in other words, they remain relatively soft until the late teens. The arch of the foot, with training, can continue to increase until the bones have fully matured. Going on pointe too early can disrupt this process and permanently injure the foot.

Also, the child must be taking at least three classes a week before pointe is added to her schedule. With the addition, initially, of one full class on pointe, these four classes will ensure a correct progression and maintenance of the technique. However, a half hour of pointe after the technique class serves as well as a specially scheduled pointe class.

For the student who simply enjoys dance, without thoughts of becoming a professional, three classes a week are sufficient. The career-track student will eventually take a daily ballet class wearing old pointe shoes (too soft for pointe work) instead of regular soft slippers, and will probably do part of each class on pointe.

Although we are discussing ballet training, I need to reiterate that even those children who are clearly on the ballet track should supplement their knowledge of dance with classes in modern dance and jazz. These will both broaden the students' vocabulary base and inform each other, making the students better dancers.

TRAINING BOYS

In the preparatory stages, the technique for boys and girls is the same. In most professional schools, boys and girls attend different classes, with female teachers teaching girls and male teachers teaching boys. Unfortunately, in most studios there are not enough boys enrolled to warrant a separate class. However, boys may initially attend classes for reasons other than learning to dance — the dance studio is a great place to meet girls. One studio that had a substantial male enrollment decided to form a special class for the boys, only to see them give up dancing because the reason for their attendance was taken away! Nevertheless, at the intermediate level boys need to develop specific technical skills, and a class geared to their requirements is beneficial. Male dancers need training that will not only develop a high jump but also give them the strength to lift a partner. The class for male dancers is therefore designed to emphasize strength-building. There are also some marked differences in the execution of turns; the male dancer does not have to rise on pointe, so he performs a windup action as the turn begins. This type of action is not part of the female dancer's training.

Additionally, the masculine style of presentation — how the dancer holds himself, how he walks or stands — is very different from the feminine style. If a male teacher is not available for a boys class at a school, the female teacher must be aware of these differences and make sure that the boys in her class develop the correct style. Attending dance performances and watching ballet videos will provide some additional guidance to the young boy. So much of the young dancer's training relies on osmosis, so seeing the right role models will prompt him to imitate the correct style.

Because they are so scarce in the dance field, boys may be expected to perform movements for which their musculature has not been adequately prepared and that may be physically harmful. Just as girls should not be put on pointe too early, boys must not be allowed to lift their partners before their back and leg muscles are up to the task. (Again it is hard to provide a specific age because physiques differ so widely; a fourteen-year-old with a strong musculature may be able to perform some lifts that an eighteen-year-old with a frail physique cannot engage in safely.)

Although schools give scholarships more readily to boys than to girls, the more talented are still all too easily lured by the more prestigious schools. As with girls, parents should guard against the exploitive aspects of the dance world and consider their child's emotional and physical welfare, especially when scholarship offers include the need to send the child away from home.

However, boys can typically start dancing at a later age than girls and still excel in ballet, modern dance, and jazz. Many male modern dancers do not discover dance until their college years. Rudolf Nureyev (1938–1993) is the most stellar example of a ballet dancer who started training when he was seventeen.

JUDGING A YOUNG DANCER'S POTENTIAL

It is not surprising that parents should want to know if their child has the ability and talent to pursue a career in dance when the life of the family is affected at every turn by the demands of the studio. The daily ballet class is augmented by other types of lessons like pointe, character, or jazz as well as, in some studios, modern dance and tap. Rehearsal for performances can consume a tremendous amount of time. Most large studios mount a production of *The Nutcracker*, at Christmastime and, of course, the end-of-the-year recital requires lengthy preparations. With all of these activities, not only the child's but the whole family's life seems to revolve around the dance studio.

Probably more than in any other art form, success in dance is dependent upon the physical makeup of the individual. Of course, the right physique is not enough, but it does provide the vehicle for all other necessary qualities. The ability to see a movement or position and transpose it accurately onto your body is very important and is the first step in kinesthenic awareness. Musicality is another necessary quality, aided by some training in music (classes in solfège or piano) to help train the ear. But above all, there must be a desire to dance. Many dancers with less-than-perfect instruments grace our stages. My first teacher, Olga Preobrazhenskaya, was regularly thrown out of Marius Petipa's class, in part because she was short and had rounded shoulders. Petipa called her an ugly monkey and a hunchback, but she persevered, took other classes, and returned to his studio unabashed. She became one of the leading ballerinas of her era.

Parents should not expect the dance teacher to be a soothsayer and predict the student's future. Being in the right place at the right time also figures in the development of a successful career. Clear, unquestionable talent is very rare and often works against the student unless it is accompanied by an equally clear will to become a dancer. In other words, a child with great physical facility will often not work as hard as a less well endowed one and, as a result, will not develop the necessary strength or precision.

The progression in the acquisition of technique is a steady and measured one, with each consecutive year of study supplying specific information that is built upon in the following year. This yearly progression prepares the musculature and develops motor control as the child grows, allowing for the gradual learning of necessary skills and a refinement in the execution of all technical aspects.

We must distinguish between learning a trick and learning a technique. Tricks are shortcuts that apply to a particular situation; they do not enlarge our knowledge of the technique, nor do they transfer to other areas of learning. Technique, on the other hand, is a cumulative process in which each step leads logically to the next, and the expertise learned in one area relates to all other areas of the activity.

SUMMER WORKSHOPS

When a child is old enough and proficient enough to benefit from continuing studies during the summer months (generally around age twelve), she or he has several options. The teacher may recommend a workshop at a pre-professional school or, if your dance school remains open, that your child continue to attend classes there. Many summer programs around the country provide excellent instruction and an opportunity for dancers to experience a new teaching approach. Your choice of program will be guided by your teacher's recommendation, which in turn depends on her or his affiliation. A school that favors the Balanchine style may suggest Seattle or New York's School of American Ballet , while a Russian-method school will lean toward San Francisco or the Joffrey Ballet programs, or even Houston, which is influenced by the English technique.

There is one unquestionable advantage to attending summer workshops: the opportunity for children to meet and dance with students from different parts of the country, and thus to gauge their levels of proficiency by national standards. However, a number of questions should be asked before you decide to send your child to a summer program. Is the child emotionally mature enough to fully enjoy and benefit from the experience? Is her level of proficiency high enough to enable her to take full advantage of the session? Is the program's method sufficiently in harmony with the current instruction, so that the student's understanding of the technique will be enhanced?

This last question is of particular importance. If the summer program has a different technical basis than the home school, the two teachers will obviously be working against each other to the student's detriment. If the method of instruction is very different from what the student knows, the student will not have the opportunity to test and fully integrate the newfound knowledge.

Additionally, students may sustain some injuries from working in a style very different from that of the home school. For example, if the summer faculty stresses a perfect 180-degree turnout while the home school is not as emphatic about it, the student may put too much pressure on the knee and ankle joints in straining to achieve the newly demanded position. Or, if the height of the leg in extensions is emphasized, students may sacrifice their alignment in striving to reach the desired height. For all of these concerns, the home teacher is the best source of information. He or she knows your child's strengths and weaknesses and can direct her or him to a program that is both conducted at the right level of proficiency and philosophically in harmony with the home school's method.

Your child's emotional maturity is also very important. In professional schools, on the East Coast in particular, an enormous emphasis is placed on the right physique and weight, especially for girls. Comparing herself to other students in the class, the child may become dissatisfied and feel rejected because she is not getting the attention that thinner girls command. This may lead her to adopt an unreasonable diet regimen that is detrimental to both her physical health and her psyche. (We will speak in more detail on this subject in chapter 7.) A young dancer faces rejection, real or imagined, almost daily: the teacher did not correct her as much as other classmates; others received more accolades; she was not chosen for a part in a production. It is important to choose a program that builds students' self-confidence in a loving environment.

And finally, is the child physically prepared to cope with the rigorous schedule of the summer workshop? If the student has been taking class three times a week, how will her or his body respond to four classes a day?

Besides the professional summer workshops in dance only, numerous summer camps throughout the country emphasize the arts. These offer a worthwhile alternative for children under fourteen who enjoy dancing but are not necessarily planning to become dancers. In these programs, besides dance classes, the children can enjoy art lessons, swimming, and nature walks as well as other athletic and nonathletic activities. The pressure to excel in dance is generally not present, and the experience can be very positive.

. . .

Of course, no single formula is going to address the needs of all dance students. Ideally, a child begins serious dance studies at the age of seven or eight with one class a week. Some schools will expect the second-year student to attend two classes weekly, with the commitment growing to a daily class by age twelve or thirteen. For the recreational student, fewer classes may be adequate. All students over the age of twelve may add other techniques to their curricula; thus pointe, modern dance, jazz, character, and partnering incrementally supplement the ballet class.

It must be remembered that improving technique and keeping the body "primed" require practice. This can only be achieved in class. Even professional dancers rely on a teacher to lead them through a class. Therefore, progression through a dance curriculum demands regular attendance at the scheduled classes.

Student of the Chicago Academy for the Arts.
©1997 Mitchell Canoff

⚡ 5 ⚡

What to Wear

F OR DANCERS, it is hard to imagine the world prior to Lycra. Today's basic classroom dancewear generally consists of a leotard
and tights made of nonrestrictive stretch fabric, from Lycra to cotton,
that conforms to the body and allows comfort and ease of movement.
But such congenial dress did not always exist.

   In the nineteenth century, a costumier at the Paris Opera, Mons.
Maillot, invented tights and gave his name to his invention. However,
maillots were expensive, as well as bulky (if made of cotton) or fragile
(if made of silk). Until the latter part of the nineteenth century, female
dancers wore tutus in class, and male dancers wore pants and shirts.
Teachers taught in street clothes. Cecchetti, the Italian teacher, de-
rided female teachers because they could not demonstrate the movements, encumbered as they were by their long skirts and petticoats.
Most female teachers of the late nineteenth and early twentieth cen-
turies taught sitting in a chair. As late as the 1940s, Mme. Rosanne, a
very popular teacher at the studio Wacker in Paris, conducted class
from an armchair. As dancing became more athletic, the need for special practice clothes became obvious; but before the explosion in the
manufacturing of exercise clothes, dancers dressed in homemade tunics and knitted tights. On stage, they wore silk stockings. These were
extra long, designed to reach above the top of the leg and be hidden
under the tutu. They were secured by placing several coins under and

around the top periphery of the stockings, tying the coins with strings, and then gathering and tying the strings around the waist. This engineering feat produced a smooth-looking leg but was extremely uncomfortable, because the strings cut into the flesh with every motion.

The leotard was also invented in the nineteenth century, by acrobat Jules Leotard. The prototype of this garment covered the upper thighs — not unlike the early version of the male swimsuits — and, unless expertly fitted, tended to bunch up. It was first worn by men because it was traditionally more acceptable for men than for women to reveal their legs; men's ballet costumes of this period often utilized modified versions of the leotard, while women still appeared only in tutus that descended to the knee.

A lot of lore surrounds the use of the layered, warm clothing so dear to dancers. One of the functions of layering, dancers will tell you, is to induce weight loss; the fact that water loss through sweating does not result in real weight loss is somehow glossed over and ignored. In the never-ending pursuit of thinness, dancers resort to promoting as much sweating as possible. To that end, in the faraway days of my training, we wore plastic pants under our leotards and wrapped our thighs in plastic tablecloths. One of the students cut up her mother's tablecloth for this purpose; it had a pattern of little fish, which could be seen swimming upstream under her pink tights. Today, dancers can buy all sorts of specially made wraps for every part of the body, but somehow most dancers still prefer the makeshift article, like the extra sweater tied around the waist.

Another function of the layered look, dancers maintain, is to warm the muscles. However, while legwarmers and heavy sweatshirts may help to hold the warmth generated by the body, they do not actually "oil" the muscles, as Alexandra Danilova (b.1904) likes to describe the warming process. (The first use of legwarmers is attributed to Danilova. She cut the arms off her sweater and wore them on her legs.) The deep lubrication that happens during exercise can only be generated by the body itself.

Often the layering is necessitated by circumstances. There are many idle minutes during rehearsals when the dancer loses body heat.

If the studio is cold and drafty, the extra clothing helps to keep the heat in and prevents the body from cooling down too quickly.

In a London studio where I took class regularly, the heating consisted of a coal stove that smoked when it was first lit in the morning. Our teacher would open the skylight windows in order to get rid of the smoke, and the heat rose with the smoke. We came dressed in legwarmers, heavy socks over our ballet shoes, sweaters, and sometimes, on particularly cold days, woolen hats and mittens. As class progressed, the smoke evaporated, the skylight was shut, the room warmed up, and we shed various articles of clothing until we looked less like bag people and more like dancers.

The final function of layering is disguise. Dancers will swath to hide some real or imagined deficiency, as well as real or imagined extra weight. For example, a dancer with an instep that is underdeveloped will wear heavy socks or legwarmers bunched up over the feet; another who is self-conscious about her posterior will drape a sweatshirt around her waist. The idea is that what you cannot see does not exist. Under these circumstances, a teacher needs x-ray eyes to give accurate corrections.

Dance attire is designed not only to provide as much freedom of motion as possible, but also to allow the teacher a clear view of the body for corrections. Teachers routinely demand the shedding of unnecessary layers. Some dance schools have rigid dress codes that make it possible for the teacher to demand specific attire; but as students get older, this enforcement becomes more and more difficult.

Basically, a female dancer needs only tights, a leotard, and shoes. If the weather is cold, a pair of legwarmers, socks with the toes and heels cut off so that they can be worn over the shoes, and a sweatshirt will make the student more comfortable. Boys need a good athletic belt, tights, and a t-shirt. Often young boys are more at ease in sweatpants instead of the all-revealing tights. However, sweatshirts and pants conceal too much of the body and thus hinder the teacher in correcting motions. Both boys and girls need a strong piece of elastic to hold their tights or sweatpants in place; although tights have an elasticized waistband, it is generally not strong enough to keep the tights pulled up.

Light colors are best because they are more revealing. It is easier to see a muscle under a pair of pink (for girls) or gray (for boys) tights than under a pair of black ones. Schools generally have specific colors for each class level or age. This practice gives homogeneity to the class and eliminates any distraction that a riot of colors would produce. When color is not specified, a solid-colored leotard is best. Leotards designed for aerobics, with bright patterns and high-cut legs or bare midriffs, are not suitable.

The style of the leotard also depends on the season. In summer, short sleeves or no sleeves are fine, but in the colder months, long-sleeved leotards are best. The leotard must fit well: it must not be so large that it bunches around the waist or hips, but must not be so short that the student is forever yanking at it. Remember that the whole attire is designed to provide the least amount of distraction and the greatest amount of comfort, allowing the student to concentrate fully on the motions.

Wearing jewelry in class is also discouraged by most teachers, although little post earrings are usually tolerated. The reason for this prohibition is safety. Should a hand inadvertently smack into another person, a ring, bracelet, or watch can become a lethal weapon. Necklaces or chains bounce around when students are jumping and, again, are a hazard, especially in partnering classes. Generally, it is best to come to class unadorned.

To avoid unnecessary purchases, it is always a good idea to determine what the teacher or school will allow the students to wear. For example, wraparound skirts are pretty and children love to wear them, but not every school allows them to be worn in class.

SHOES

Shoes are probably the most important item on the dancer's clothing list. Soft slippers, for both boys and girls, must hug the foot: you cannot buy slippers that allow for growth, especially if the shoes are made of leather, which stretches with use. Unlike regular shoes, the sole of a dance slipper does not extend all the way to the end of the toes or the heel. If the shoe is of inferior quality, its lining will sometimes bunch up at the seam located right under the metatarsals the area of the foot where the dancer stands on half-pointe. This bunching is not only un-comfortable; it can actually cause alignment problems, because the student will shift his or her weight off that area in order to avoid the pressure. Therefore, when buying shoes, check for a smooth seam be-tween the sole and the lining. Also be sure to have the student try on the shoes wearing tights, or socks of a similar weight, for a perfect fit.

Elastic straps secure soft ballet shoes to the dancer's feet. Although some shoes come with elastics attached, in my experience these elastics are usually sewn over the front part of the instep and thus do not en-sure against heel slippage. The correct place can be found by folding the heel of the shoe forward over the insole; the elastic should be sewn at the fold.

There are many different ballet shoes on the market today. Leather slippers last longer than canvas ones. Young children usually outgrow their shoes before any real wear-and-tear-occurs, so canvas shoes will suffice for them. Some schools recommend specific brands, especially in pointe shoes. At the school where I teach, we have instituted a shoe-and-leotard pool for the very young students. Outgrown articles of dance clothing are donated to the school to be passed on to children who need them. This practice has somewhat eased the financial burden of keeping the student correctly shod.

POINTE SHOES

The fit of the pointe shoe is of the greatest importance for correct alignment and proper development of the foot. At the age of eleven, the day after I joined the ranks of the Petits Rats (dance students at the Paris Opera School) feeling very grown-up, I went to buy my first pair of pointe shoes. Unfortunately, I did not ask anyone's advice and pur-chased the most comfortable pair of shoes. The vamp was too low and the fit too loose. The shoe did not provide enough support on pointe, and I was miserable until I was fitted properly sometime later. As with soft ballet shoes, there are many brands and styles of pointe shoes, dif-fering in hardness and in the support they provide to the foot. The vamp (the upper part of the shoe), should come well above the toe phalanges (metatarsals), and for beginners, the tip should be well squared-off, providing a wide surface on which to balance. Additionally, even shoes of the same size and brand may not be exactly alike; therefore, when trying on shoes, ask the salesperson to bring several pairs. Many dancewear stores are staffed by dancers who will not object to your request. But even if you encounter resistance from the salesperson, insist until you are shown an adequate selection. As with soft slippers, wear the tights that are worn in class or socks of a similar weight when trying on the shoes.

Ballet shoes should fit tightly, not slip easily over the heel. Lambs-wool is the only toe protection a beginner requires; avoid the manufactured toe pads that are sold, as they usually add too much bulk inside the shoe and are made of material, such as plastic, that does not breathe. Advanced dancers usually do not wear anything extra in their shoes; at most, a small piece of paper towel covers the toes to prevent slippage. Newspaper is also an excellent cover. Finally, toenails should be clipped short enough so that the pad at the tip of the toe is the only part of the toe that comes in contact with the shoe when the dancer stands on pointe.

Ribbons secure pointe shoes to the dancer's feet. As soon as possible, sewing the ribbons should become the responsibility of the dancer. Sewing the ribbons by machine is fine, although it only takes minutes to sew them by hand. In the days of my training, we were required to darn the tips of our shoes; not only did the darning with thick cotton provide extra protection to the toes, but it also extended the life of the pointe shoes and provided traction.

To secure the ribbons to the shoe, fold the heel of the shoe forward over the insole and place the ribbon just beyond the crease, slightly angled toward the shoe tip. Fold the ribbon end over once to form a short hem, with the matte surface facing toward the foot. Then sew all the way around the ribbon edge with fairly small stitches, avoiding sewing over the pull string. When tying the shoe, cross the ribbons high over the instep and wrap them twice around the ankle, immediately above the ankle bone. Knot the ribbons on the inner side of the ankle twice, and tuck the ends under the wrapped part. When putting on the shoes for the first time, you may find that the ribbons are too long. If so, wrap them around the ankle and knot them before you cut off the excess.

Additional protection against heel slippage can be gained by sewing elastic at the heel to wrap over the instep. In use, the elastic is partially hidden by the ribbons. However, if the shoe is properly fitted, this elastic will not be necessary. Many dancers protect against slippage by simply wetting the inside of the heel and rubbing a little rosin on it before putting on the shoes.

Parents can take certain preliminary measures to help prepare their child to dance on pointe comfortably. The skin of the dancer's toes must be hardened somewhat to withstand the inevitable rubbing within the shoes. A daily application of rubbing alcohol after a shower or bath will help toughen the skin of the toes. Another approach instead of hardening the skin is to put cream on your feet regularly to keep the skin supple and prevent blisters. As extra protection, a pad made of moleskin can protect areas that are most vulnerable, like the heel or the second toe (if it is longer than the big toe). Corn pads are also useful for protecting the second toe. If a blister develops, the area should be disinfected and the toe wrapped in moleskin. Moleskin, unlike regular bandages, does not have a pad in the middle; it adheres directly to the sore. It must be left in place until it falls off, about seven to ten days; your child can shower or take a bath with it on. The blister under the moleskin will heal in that space of time, and the bandage will peel off easily without hurting the skin. Moleskin can even be applied to broken skin, provided that the blister has been thoroughly disinfected.

HAIR

Securing the hair away from the face and neck allows a clear view of the neck area. The neck position permits teachers to make important alignment diagnoses, alerting them to problems further down the spine. Both girls and boys with long hair need to keep their hair off their face and neck. A headband or ponytail is usually sufficient for boys to achieve that goal. For girls, one of the easiest ways to deal with long hair is to braid it and then pin the braid up or secure it with barrettes. Another way of securing hair begins with a ponytail with a ribbon tied at the tip; the hair is rolled into a bundle until the elastic securing the ponytail is reached, then the ribbon is tied over the elastic. Any manner of putting the hair up for class is acceptable as long as the hair does not come down in class.

My teacher was adamant about hair staying in place and shoe ribbons remaining tied. If you were unlucky enough to have either of these calamities occur during class, you were instantly dismissed and forced to sit out the rest of the class in disgrace. In this country, teachers tend to be less harsh in their treatment of students, but such leniency should not be an invitation to laxity. Ultimately, students do not learn as well when they are distracted by hair falling all over their face.

A List of Necessities

Girls

Tights

Leotard

Shoes

Elastic for the waist

Elastic bands, hairpins, hairnet, ribbons for the hair

Safety pins

Boys

Tights

Socks (if tights do not have feet)

Shoes

T-shirt or sweatshirt

Elastic for the waist

Dance belt (athletic belt)

Headband or elastic bands if hair is long

Add to the list, for both girls and boys, legwarmers if the weather is cool. Parachute pants are very popular for class but are seldom allowed by teachers; they are also not as warm as woolen tights. In cool weather, an extra sweatshirt or a ballet wraparound sweater comes in handy until the body warms up. Additionally, girls dancing on pointe should always have an extra pair of pointe shoes in their bags. Too often a pair of shoes will become too soft during class, or ribbons will come unsewn. The student will then have no choice but to sit out the remainder of the class.

Before buying any accouterments, check with the school to find out what its requirements or prohibitions may be. For example, the floor in our studio is gray marly, which marks very easily, so we do not allow students to wear any black shoes. Even boys wear white or gray shoes.

Dance clothes are very expensive, and girls are often seduced by all the frilly, soft items on sale in dance stores. If these items are not allowed in class, they may be purchased as expensive play clothes.

Students of the Chicago Academy for the Arts.
©1997 Mitchell Canoff

⚹ 6 ⚹

Parent and Teacher Relations

L OUIS XIV of France understood the value of ritual. Life at his court seemed to mirror the orderliness of a choreographed dance. From the moment he awoke (attended by courtiers and dignitaries invited to witness the event) through the day (during which his every encounter was governed by strict rules of etiquette) to his retirement in the evening (again formally escorted), Louis XIV sought to establish a harmonious atmosphere in which specific rules of conduct were applied to every exchange and encounter.

Observance of rituals remains an important part of the ballet world. The size of a major company may preclude a degree of familiarity that is often found in smaller groups; usually the ballet master or choreographer of the larger company is approached with formality, and a strict hierarchy among company members prevails. A dancer seldom questions the choreographer or teacher. Complaints are filed through formal channels. The artistic director is in control of the artistic product; thus the management of a ballet company can be likened to the autocratic rule of a king.

This formal attitude toward the teacher or choreographer may be an anomaly in our culture today, yet there was a time when teachers were among the most respected members of our society. Both at the Paris Opera and at the Royal Ballet School, ballet students were expected to curtsy or bow to the teacher before and after class. Other cultures also preserve a certain decorum toward their mentors. In India the guru or dance teacher does not countenance questions. In his book *The Dance through the Ages,* Walter Sorell quotes the Indian dancer Lalli as saying, "When I ask a question, Vikram affects good nature but reminds me that a student's question is a sign of little faith in the teacher."

ATTENDANCE AND PUNCTUALITY

In contrast to the state schools in Europe where students do not pay for instruction, open studios and private dance schools place the teacher in the position of having to please the students and parents. My teacher at the Paris Opera could refuse to allow students to participate in the class; the Paris Opera Ballet School is a state institution. Students accepted into the program attend without charge and are also beholden, under an unwritten contract, to fulfill their obligations: to attend classes, perform when required, and abide by the rules of the institution. In this country, parents pay for the privilege of having their children instructed. However, too often they feel that this entitles them to take liberties.

The parent who drives the child to class is ultimately responsible for the child's punctuality. For the teacher to punish a tardy child by forbidding participation seems eminently unfair. However, this action is motivated by concern for the well-being of the student. Ballet class is a continuum, with each exercise following the previous one in a logical sequence that engages every muscle of the body cumulatively. The exercises are designed to warm the body gradually as well as impart kinetic information. A child who has missed the first couple of exercises has missed this information and runs the risk of injury by working with muscles that have not been properly warmed up. Therefore, getting to class after it has started is not only discourteous and disruptive but also robs the student of the opportunity to experience the technique in the logical manner in which it is presented.

Arriving on time has one further benefit: it provides the opportunity to make an effective transition from the outside world of traffic jams, crowded buses, noise, and confusion to the meditative state of heightened self-awareness. Getting dressed for class becomes a part of the ritual, a moment of preparation that invokes the right frame of mind for sharing in the ritual of class fully and constructively. Punctuality allows the student to enter into a state of mind that is conducive to learning.

Punctuality is only one area where the parent sets the tone. A casual attitude on the part of the parent quickly communicates itself to the child and affects the way she or he accepts corrections, which has a direct impact on her or his progress. On the other hand, parents who regard the teacher as a professional who does not make up rules arbitrarily and who has the welfare of the child at heart, help to maintain the discipline necessary for their child's progress. A recent book, *Beyond the Classroom*, by Lawrence Steinberg, Bradford Brown, and Stanford Dornbusch, points to the indifference of parents as the main reason for underachievement in school. Children often reflect parental attitudes and priorities and unconsciously act them out. Furthermore, parents set criteria or expectations. "Did you have a good class?" elicits a different response than "Did you have fun?"

Learning to dance is a little different from learning how to play the piano or sing. In these disciplines, a weekly lesson is supported by individual practice. In dance, the lesson is both instruction and practice. Dancers need the vigilant eye of the teacher to catch departures from the desired line and to point out mistakes. Advanced dancers may on occasion do a barre on their own, but this is usually due to dire circumstances that prevent them from taking class. While a solitary barre warms the body and maintains the musculature, it is no substitute for regular class. In some ways, a missed class cannot be made up.

Especially in cases where an injury affects the student for a long time, the student should make an effort to observe classes. Of course, the student must be mature enough to draw some benefit from watching rather than doing. The advantages of watching class are numerous. Observation can provide new insights and understanding of the technique that can be applied when the student returns to class. It is easy to forget that dance is not only a physical activity but an intellectual one as well. In an article called "The Mental Edge" (*U.S News and World Report*, August 3, 1992) William Allman writes: "In a study published this month, neurologist Scott Grafton of the University of Southern California found that the brain learns new skills by fine-tuning the neural circuits that are involved in making the motion." Thus going over a movement "in your head" helps to enhance the actual performance of the motion.

The idea that class cannot be missed and the need to observe when unable to participate were drummed into us from an early age. During my first semester at the Royal Ballet School in London, all the new students were put under Miss Winifred Edwards's (b.1895) tutelage. It was Miss Edwards's task to imbue us with the special Royal Ballet style, restrained yet regal, with clean technical definition.

Miss Edwards was a tall, forbidding person who wore white sandals and stood in a perfect fifth position. The process of learning seemed to us more like being broken-in than being educated. Miss Edwards dismantled our little mannerisms, shortcuts, and adaptations, seeking a stark, precise execution of all movements. Besides teaching us technique, she lectured us on our diet and on how to take care of our equipment; our tunics were to be clean and pressed and our shoes scrubbed with rubbing alcohol each week to erase dirt and scuffs. We also learned how to darn the tips of our pointe shoes to prolong their hardness and guard against slipping. Every Monday morning, we stood in a row in front of Miss Edwards holding our supply of shoes out for her inspection, quaking lest our weekend scrubbing session appear to have been less than perfect.

Because the schedule and technique taught at the Royal Ballet School were more demanding than what many students had previously known, several could not stand the strain. Toward the end of the semester, 50 percent of the students no longer attended class. Two weeks before the semester break, I twisted my ankle coming down from a small jump. I returned to school to observe classes, hobbling with the aid of a cane.

This time off proved invaluable. Not only did I sit in on the classes that I would regularly have attended, but I snuck in to observe other teachers. My favorites were Errol Addison (1903–1983) and Harold Turner (1908–1962). Mr. Addison, a small, jovial man, was a wonderful spinner and passed on the secrets of good pirouettes to his students.

I had been a tentative turner at best, but after listening to Mr. Addison and watching his directives, I began to understand the dynamics of the motion. Mr. Turner was no less a showman, a little more distant and at times sarcastic. He always wore white to teach, his balding head gleaming as if freshly scrubbed. He was more precise technically than Addison was, but he still had a keen sense of drama and bravado. I returned to my own class with new enthusiasm, insight, and appreciation for the technique.

VOLUNTEER WORK AND STUDENT ADVANCEMENT

Many schools rely on the volunteer work of mothers to organize a variety of adjunct activities. These may include printing programs and tickets, arranging refreshments for the intermission at performances, answering the phone during class sessions, or running fundraising events. I have asked several teachers how they feel about this, and their overwhelming response was that, although they are grateful for the dedication and real help that such parents provide, volunteer work does not entitle parents to dictate policy or interfere with the running of the school in any substantive way. However, teachers welcome input from parents when it concerns scheduling as well as individual problems that may arise.

While pre-professional ballet companies are generally nonprofit organizations, they still must be operated as businesses in the sense of keeping within a specified budget. Teachers like to hear comments, complaints, and concerns that allow them to provide a better service to their student body. Therefore, communication between teacher and parent is essential. When the need for a conversation arises, the best approach is to arrange an appointment when neither teacher nor parent will be rushed and the matter can be discussed in a congenial atmosphere.

Enid Lynn, Director of the Hartford School of Ballet, has brought up another point. Children studying dance are bound to feel disappointment at one time or another, perhaps because they did not get a part they wanted in a performance or were not placed in a higher-level class. Ms. Lynn says, "It is my hope that parents do not project their own disappointment to their children." She cites one incident when a mother insisted that because her daughter was not accepted into the pre-professional program, she would not return to the school. The child was heartbroken. In this case, the mother relented and brought the child to the open-enrollment program. Not every child is capable of becoming a professional, and to deny them dance classes for that reason is rather shortsighted. A child should have the opportunity to draw on the benefits of a dance education without the pressure of having to excel or commit to a career.

At the other end of the scale from the overly ambitious parent is the one who constantly reminds the teacher in front of the child that the child is not going to be a dancer. At the same time, the parent demands steady improvement and perceivable hard work. The child, in this case, receives mixed messages: on the one hand, the parent says that dance lessons are rather frivolous, but on the other hand, the parent expects dedication and discipline. In one particular case, the child was very talented but also rather lazy. Because of the parent's attitude, the child progressed only because of innate ability and never reached her full potential.

Jan Snow, who runs a studio and pre-professional company, the Garden City Ballet in Missoula, Montana, is adamant about the involvement of parents in technical decisions: "If you have researched the studio you are sending your child to, then don't presume that you know more than the teacher and try to tell them what to do or when your child should advance to the next level." Teachers do not arbitrarily decide that one child should advance and another should not; they have the best interest of the child in mind when they make this kind of decision. And in cases where there are two tracks, as at the Hartford School of Ballet, the teacher can save the child a lot of disappointment in the long run by directing her or him into an open-enrollment program. Children who are in the wrong class soon fall behind their classmates, class becomes a chore, and the most important aspect of dancing is lost: the pure joy of movement.

Some teachers are reluctant to accept students who have studied in other schools. They maintain that, besides coming with all sorts of bad habits in the execution of the technique, if the student was dissatisfied at the previous studio she or he will eventually be dissatisfied with them, too. Although this attitude may seem extreme, and some students have a legitimate reason for switching teachers, there are instances when the move is motivated by reasons other than the welfare and education of the child. Most teachers will tell a parent when it is time to seek another teacher, generally because their program no longer provides what the child needs to progress.

Only in this country has the idea taken hold that the more teachers the student studies with, the better. In the older traditions that are still followed in Europe and Russia, dancers study with one primary teacher for several years and may only have had a total of two teachers by the time they reach a pre-professional level. In professional schools, students study with a primary teacher and experience other teachers only when studying other subjects, like character or pointe.

The process of learning is always an active one. As a young, inexperienced teacher, I readily blamed the teacher for a student's bad technique. I have come to realize that the teacher can only present the material and insist on correct execution. I have often been humbled by students whose innate kinetic response was so beautiful that I could only gaze at them and wonder how they knew what they knew. In several instances, I felt that an old dancer's soul was hiding in the young body; my role was to bring to consciousness all that the child already knew. A teacher, no matter how brilliant, cannot make a student into a dancer. Students bring into the studio their raw talent and active interest. The teacher provides the tools for fashioning an instrument — out of a sometimes unwilling body — that, with training, will become flexible, responsive, and graceful. It is the teacher's responsibility to provide the correct tool; a screwdriver will not do when a hammer is needed. The student's responsibility is to use the tool appropriately and to become ever more adept in its applications.

One of the most important ingredients in this process is trust. Both parent and child must trust that the teacher knows what is needed to ensure the child's progress. If you have doubts, ask questions, look at other studios, and change teachers if you are convinced that your teacher is not providing the necessary training. But do not blame your child's lack of progress arbitrarily on the teacher.

REHEARSALS

Probably the most difficult periods in the life of a studio are the weeks of rehearsal prior to a performance. During that time, patience and understanding must be exercised by all. Rehearsal is not like a class, with a definite structure and a prescribed set of movements to cover. Choreography has two stages: first, the learning of the steps, and second, the practice to perfect the dance. The dance is remembered and perfected only through repetition. Rehearsals may run overtime because any one section of the dance must be firmly fixed in the memory in order to be remembered at the next rehearsal. There is nothing more wasteful than to have students forget the material covered from one rehearsal to the next. This is like running on the same spot.

Once the students have committed the steps to memory, the real work of perfecting the dance begins. The attitude "I know the dance, I don't have to attend rehearsal" is misguided. Perfecting the execution is an endless task; only through complete familiarity with the technical material can the spirit of the dance emerge. Additionally, every single performer is critical to the whole. In a group dance, performers rely on each other for the correct spacing; when students are missing, the others must imagine the space that would be occupied. This is a hard task, especially for neophytes.

The very format of rehearsals invites frayed nerves. Unlike class, rehearsals do not involve all dancers all of the time. Sitting out while a section is being completed may be boring, but the student must nevertheless sit quietly, without talking, so as not to distract either the choreographer or the other dancers. The cooperation of all participants, either active or passive, is essential to the smooth and efficient running of a rehearsal.

. . .

Even if your child is not considering a career in dance, the discipline of adhering to specific rules will establish a disciplined attitude toward other activities. The study of dance helps children become more studious students and more directed professionals in their chosen field.

In every situation, there is an appropriate behavior that suits the occasion. The process of educating children includes the recognition that we impose certain restraints on ourselves in order to function in the world. We do not, as a rule, allow our children to play hide-and-seek among the pews during a church service, or play basketball in the living room, or put their feet on the table during dinner. Rules established by society often disregard the individual expression in favor of communal comfort and safety. Similarly, the rules of behavior at dance studios are concerned with creating room for introspection in a receptive atmosphere.

Students of the Chicago Academy for the Arts.
©1997 Mitchell Canoff

✖ 7 ✖

Recitals, Demonstrations, and Concerts

PERFORMANCE is often the main justification for all our hard work. In performance we realize truths that may escape us in the studio. The anticipation of performance keeps us interested, and the memory of the last performance sustains us and reinforces the necessity of keeping our instrument tuned. But is performing an essential part of the experience of learning to dance?

Performance completes our understanding of dance. It puts our long hours of practice into perspective and gives us an opportunity to share what we know and what we feel with others. It is a vital part of learning to dance because, through the experience, we learn how to draw pleasure by giving pleasure to others, as well as nourish certain aspects of our personality that crave that kind of attention. Many dancers say that they feel most vital, most alive while dancing. Violette Verdy, speaking of Nureyev, said: "Maybe he did not get to the Absolute, but he kept going there. . . . His most purest, his everything was his dancing. Not because he was privileged, but because he gave everything" (interview with Russell D. Baker, University of Utah Department of Ballet Newsletter, Winter 1993).

At the Paris Opera Ballet School, performance opportunities came early. We were cast as pages (walk-on parts) in operas and ballets. Operatic stories were our mythology, and to be part of the panoply was magic. During the day we were ordinary schoolchildren studying grammar and arithmetic; in the afternoon we attended ballet class and rehearsal; but in the evening we stepped into a fairyland world of heroes.

My first role, at age eleven, was that of a page in Guiseppe Verdi's (1813–1901) *Otello*. I carried a casket of jewels to Desdemona, knelt in front of her as she sang her aria while admiring the jewels, and then retreated backward into the wings. I remember vividly the excitement of preparing for the performance — putting on the makeup and long blond wig — and standing quietly in the wings before stepping into the magical, lighted space. A silence of completion seemed to envelop me as I walked in measured steps toward Desdemona.

As we grew older, we were cast in walk-on parts in different operas. In some operas we actually danced: in Verdi's *Aida*, we were Blackamoors and then slaves in the Grand Procession; in Hector Berlioz's (1803–1869) *The Damnation of Faust*, we were Blessed Spirits, and then Devils. While the dance of the Devils was exciting, I preferred the dance of the Spirits, because the music was quietly evocative and our movements were soft, almost trancelike. My favorite opera was Charles Gounod's (1818–1893) *Romeo and Juliet*. Standing upstage, I marveled at Juliet's beauty as the chorus sang her praises in the first act, and I wept as she drank the poison in the third act. But Gounod's *Faust* best personified our growth and progress; we began as children among the crowd in the first act, and graduated to the ballet. We also took part in ballets such as Harald Lander's (1905–1971) *Etudes*, Mikhail Fokine's *Petrushka* and Serge Lifar's (1905–1986) *La Valse*. The choreography in these works was designed for our competence — Lander and Lifar personally taught us our parts — and one ballet was choreographed specifically for students, Albert Aveline's (1883–1968) *Jeux d'Enfants*, which was performed on special occasions.

The stage fueled my imagination, but I also learned an important lesson: to be fully accepting of my place within the whole; to realize, as the old cliché says, that there are no small parts. Every individual on stage fulfills an important role in the overall production, and the little girl kneeling for a few minutes at the feet of the diva is an integral part of the picture.

When major ballet companies come to the city, they sometimes require supers or extras as they are known in the movies, to complete their productions. Our students are often chosen for walk-on parts in *Swan Lake* or *Sleeping Beauty*. The experience is exciting and instructive, and the students invariably return to the studio newly inspired and motivated.

TYPES OF PERFORMANCES

Professional schools affiliated with a company usually mount a production of *The Nutcracker* at Christmastime. Well-established schools may have a junior company, composed of the most advanced students, that performs at social functions as well as at other schools and that mounts an occasional performance of its own. For many schools, however, the end-of-the-year recital is the only venue for performance. This recital serves several functions. It provides an opportunity for parents to see the student body in its entirety and to witness their child's progress within the larger context of other classes. It provides an outlet for the students' self-expression and a focus for the classwork. It is also a social occasion that brings parents together and engenders feelings of loyalty and support — a feeling of belonging to an exclusive club. How schools refer to the performance may indicate the breadth and formality of the presentation. Each of the common appellations — recital, demonstration, and concert — has a connotation that reveals its focus.

Recitals

Recitals vary both in scope and in length. Schools appreciate the fact that parents want to see their own children perform, and they try to provide every student with the opportunity for a solo. Generally the school rents an auditorium or theatre for the performance and, to offset the cost, charges parents a performance and a costume fee.

A serious drawback of the recital is that too often rehearsals take up class time beginning (as they often do) in the second semester. While students are learning routines, they are not improving their technique; when half a year is spent on preparing for a performance rather than on regular study, the technical aspects of training are sadly neglected.

Nevertheless, the recital is popular with many schools as well as with parents and students, and it fulfills the need for performance experience.

A demonstration usually describes a less formal presentation limited to showing the students' classwork. However, it is not an impromptu affair. The demonstration consists of material from the lessons that has been selected and arranged into a choreographed whole to represent what the students have been working on all year. It may also include some choreographed dances performed by the senior students as a finale.

As in the recital, each student is involved in the performance, and rehearsals may take place during regular class time. The demonstration does not detract from working on technique because the elements rehearsed are the same as those that would regularly be practiced. If the senior students are to perform a dance as a finale to the performance, it is usually rehearsed after the regular lesson is finished.

The format of the demonstration allows parents not only to see their own child's progress but also to witness the progression of the technique through different levels. In many ways, the demonstration is an educational experience for both parents and children. The students have the opportunity to see other classes and get some idea of where their training is leading them. The parents get an overview of the training their child is receiving and gain an appreciation of the technique as it unfolds through the years of study.

Another advantage of the demonstration is that it is usually a low-budget affair. While it may be necessary to rent an auditorium, the cost is generally covered by charging a modest ticket price. Also, there is no costume fee because the students perform in their classroom attire. The most significant advantage of the demonstration, however, is that it does not interrupt training to make time for rehearsals.

A concert generally involves only the senior students of the school and is composed of choreographed works (usually short ballets).

Some schools mount full-length productions of classics like *Coppelia* or *Cinderella*. Rehearsals are scheduled separately from class time and often require the students to give up their weekends and many evenings.

Mounting a production requires many hours of work, not only in rehearsal time but in production time as well — designing the scenery, making the costumes, planning the lighting, arranging publicity and promotion. The group assembled for the duration functions as a professional company with a clear delineation of duties and responsibilities. The director of the school may commission a choreographer to mount the ballet or hire professional dancers for the principal roles. The experience for the students involved in such a production is invaluable. It duplicates the process of a professional company and allows the students to determine whether the life of a dancer is really what they want.

Although your primary reason for attending a presentation is to see your own child dance, you must realize that every parent is there for the same reason. You must not be unduly disappointed if your child appears only for a few minutes. The teacher's selection of the students is based on their proficiency, with an eye to creating a harmonious whole. For the child, the experience includes the anticipation and preparation for the performance, the excitement of waiting in the wings, and the applause at the end. Even if students are on stage for only two minutes, they will still experience the cumulative magic of the event.

Pre-professional Experience

Many schools establish performing groups to give their students an opportunity to gain performance experience at a pre-professional level. This experience is very valuable in the education of the dancer; it fosters the development of a stage presence and a firsthand realization of what being a dancer entails. In performance, the dancer realizes that technique is not enough; style and stage presence are also necessary. Performances need not be on a grand scale to be instructive. Whenever dancers step out in front of an audience — whether performing in a gym for elementary schoolchildren, or on a makeshift stage in a cafeteria for senior citizens — they are tapping into their artistic potential and transcending their technical levels.

A dancer must be able to communicate the enjoyment of motion to the audience. A technically brilliant performance without feeling leaves the audience cold. Ultimately, such a performance, even with its amazing technical feats, is boring to watch. On the other hand, a technically flawed performance that is full of feeling may be a much more satisfying experience. Of course, we always hope for performances that are satisfying in both respects; a brilliant technique becomes the vehicle for a full emotional expression.

Competition

Many studios subscribe to various competitions around the country. These competitions usually offer a weekend of master classes with distinguished teachers and culminate in performances by participating groups.

Studios that have a performing group often belong to the National Association of Regional Ballet (NARB). The guidelines for membership in the association stipulate that the company must be a nonprofit organization separate from the school; it must have its own Board of Directors and a budget that is not tied to the operation of the studio; and it must present one major concert a year.

At the NARB's annual national conference, companies present works for adjudication. These competitions focus more on companies than on individual dancers, so many aspiring choreographers get their start by presenting works in this venue. For the student, this format removes much of the pressure and the sense of individual rivalry that can arise when solo performances are emphasized.

Established professional schools also have the option of attending international ballet competitions, which meet in places like Varna, Bulgaria (the site of the original competition); Lausanne, Switzerland; Jackson, Mississippi; and Paris. These competitions are highly publicized and require a very high level of proficiency on the part of the competitors. Dancers usually train for them throughout the year, practicing the required variations or pas de deux. These competitions provide significant visibility to the dancers who qualify as finalists.

These venues provide additional performance experience, and the heightened pressures inherent in these situations often lead students to discover aspects of their personalities that were not apparent before: What is my response to pressure? Am I at my best when seriously challenged? Can I rise to the occasion, or do I want to run and hide?

Additionally, because these competitions attract dancers from all over the world, they provide an excellent forum for measuring one's own standard against an international norm.

COMPETITIVENESS

Dance is inherently competitive. Dancers will usually compare themselves to others in the class and strive to emulate or best those who possess qualities that they feel they lack. This type of healthy competition spurs the students to excel and improve. However, when competition is actively encouraged by the studio or the parent, it begins to act as a barrier between students and their classmates and breeds an unsuitable atmosphere.

We are not always chosen for the part we covet; casting in the annual production may cause some heartaches. It helps to remember that casting is less an expression of favoritism than a judgment call. Negative feelings toward the teacher or the classmates must not be encouraged; this kind of negativity only interferes with the learning process and robs the children of their power and will to improve.

My daughter, Nadia, still remembers vividly an incident that occurred when she was eleven and danced in the annual production of *The Nutcracker.* That year she had been selected as one of the eight little Pulcinellas who emerge from under the skirt of Mother Goose. She was very excited because this was a real dancing part. During one of the performances, the bonnet of Mindy, the girl next to her, became untied and, in the course of the dance, fell off. Mindy let it fall, finished the dance, and had the presence of mind to pick up the hat on her way offstage. She acted like a good little pro. But Mindy's mother, greeting the girls backstage, started screaming at Nadia, accusing her of deliberately knocking the hat off. Mindy started crying, Nadia started crying, and the mother went on screaming. Nadia believed she had indeed ruined the performance, and she felt guilty and hurt. This experience overshadowed all the other happy performances in which she had taken part.

Recently, one mother confided in me that there were two reasons why she transferred her daughter from a popular studio to another one: "The students were not getting enough attention because the classes were so big. Even worse, there was such competitiveness among the mothers. They will tell you the wrong time or day for an audition just so that their daughter will get a better chance." She called these mothers "barracudas" and the helpful, noncompetitive mothers "white whales."

While competitiveness is an unavoidable part of learning to dance, when it is encouraged by teachers or parents it begins to distract from the real work of learning and growing within the art form.

BALANCE BETWEEN PERFORMANCE AND CLASS

In order to perform, we must first rehearse. During the training years, a balance must be maintained between rehearsing and training. Rehearsal is not a substitute for class. Before the student reaches an intermediate level, she or he cannot miss classes because there are too few. When the student reaches an intermediate level she or he needs to be engaged in practicing and perfecting the technique on a daily basis; two or three classes a week are no longer sufficient for progress. Simply maintaining technique at one level is rather frustrating; it's like treading water. Your head is above the waves, but you are not getting anywhere. The daily class provides an opportunity to integrate new concepts and to perfect well-known ones. It is only through daily practice that one can achieve a high level of proficiency.

An amazing fact of the craft is that a dancer can perform a simple motion, such as a battement tendu — which is only a simple stretching of the leg with the toes and instep ending in an arched position — and after forty years of practice still discover new features to the motion, new sensations to be integrated. The technique is extremely complex in its simplicity, but its breadth and depth are available to us only through practice. Therefore, every year of the student's dance studies is crucial to the correct development of her or his kinetic and intellectual understanding within the dance.

There is an old adage in the profession: If you miss one class, you know it; if you miss two classes, your teacher knows it; if you miss three classes, your public knows it. Schools that substitute rehearsals for classes, while obviously preparing well for the coming production, are in fact denying young dancers the opportunity to maintain their technique, let alone progress. While the experience of performing is a very important component of dance education, providing insights for technical growth and allowing the dancer to gain confidence and develop stage presence, rehearsal schedules must honor the requirements of the daily class and not act as a substitute. In dance companies, the day begins with class and only then proceeds to rehearsal. On performance days, when time is limited and dancers need their strength for the evening show, class takes precedence. The first years of training lay the foundation for a solid technique; the last years of training are equally vital in developing technique and preparing the dancer for the challenges of the professional world. In fact, even labeling those years as the last years of training is misleading. Dancers are in training throughout their careers, so a balance must always be maintained between performance and class.

Student of the Chicago Academy for the Arts.
©1997 Mitchell Canoff

✻ 8 ✻

Avoiding Injuries

BALLET has been much maligned as injurious to the body. Turnout and the redistribution of weight it requires do put unusual strains on the body; but apart from recreational swimming, there is no physical exercise that does not strain the body. Furthermore, the warmup process is an integral part of dance training.

Young children do not generally sustain injuries by taking dance classes. It is only in more advanced training, when the musculature has been developed and dancers push the limits of their physicality, that problems may arise. However, early training conditions the musculature to a specific response. Correct use of the musculature from the start makes the dancer less prone to injury in later years.

Other factors can also make a dancer susceptible to injury: diet, lack of rest, surrounding conditions like cold and heat, and even emotional state. Through proper diet, muscles receive the nourishment they need to function efficiently and safely, and rest helps the body to perform at its peak. Surrounding conditions cannot always be controlled, but they must be addressed with proper attire and a careful warmup period when it is very cold. Part of the discipline of dancing is the learned ability to leave problems at the door of the studio, so dancers must also learn to transcend their emotional state. By paying full attention to the task at hand, dancers will not only avoid the risk of injury, but may also find that their minds are clearer and better able to cope with problems after the class is over.

CORRECT TECHNIQUE

Most dance injuries are caused by misalignment or incorrect execution of the technique, which over time predispose the body to injury. When first selecting a school, parents should watch for a few signs that correct technique is being taught. Are the students standing straight, and does the teacher correct them when they are not? When the students stand straight, are the shoulders and hips aligned to each other, and is the head balanced over the body (with the chin neither tucked under nor thrust upward)? Does the teacher emphasize turnout from the hips and correct the students who are rolling over on their instep (pronation, a sure sign that the student is not turning out from the hips)? Pronation is the cause of many problems, including knee pain and shinsplints. Are the students taught to keep their knees over their feet when bending the knees? Does the teacher talk about alignment and line, or is the height of the leg in extensions emphasized without regard to alignment and line?

It is undeniable that some body types are better suited to dance; they have a wide range of motion as well as an innate strength that allows them to control their motions from an early age. For the majority of others, whose physique falls short of the ideal, it is important to recognize limitations and work with them intelligently. People with short ligaments need to approach the stretching process with care in order to lengthen the ligaments as they build stronger muscles to protect the joints; people with long ligaments have a wider range of motion, so they must be careful to keep aligned in order to maintain the integrity of the joints and build strength. The teacher's corrections will indicate how concerned he or she is with the issues of alignment and correct execution and, most importantly, with the specific needs of each student. Does the teacher demand the same degree of turnout from all students, or does he or she correct them individually according to their capability?

SURROUNDING CONDITIONS

While injury in the studio is not common with young children, the proper surroundings during the early years of training will enhance the learning experience. Muscles function better in a warm environment. Most studios are warm in the winter; if windows are opened, care should be taken that the cooler air does not blow directly on the students. In the summer, if air conditioning is used, the thermostat ideally will not be set below 78 degrees. The process of warming up is hampered by cool temperatures, and the muscles contract quickly when idle; therefore, a warm studio is safer for dancers in both winter and summer.

Surrounding conditions also include the floor. The surface should provide traction without being sticky, a non-slip material such as marly (linoleum is not suitable, as it is usually too slippery) or wood that has been treated with a finish that prevents slipping. Rosin is sometimes used on wooden floors but is not necessary on marly. Wetting the shoes is also a solution when dancing on a polished wood floor. The floor must also be sprung; marly laid over a concrete surface is not suitable. The importance of a sprung floor cannot be overestimated. Many injuries are caused by jumping on an unyielding floor.

Suitable barres are also essential to a well-equipped studio. The height of the barre should be set at waist level. Most studios have a double rung of barres to accommodate both tall and short students; these should be securely fastened to the walls. Free-standing barres are also suitable as long as they are really sturdy. The best kind is the homemade model made out of lengths of heavy pipes (found in plumbing-supply stores); lighter material, such as aluminum, does not provide enough support. These considerations will contribute to the students' comfort and greatly reduce the risk of injury.

COMMON PROBLEMS AND THEIR TREATMENT

Most doctors are not aware of the type of exercise that ballet training entails, and they often simply tell the patient not to dance. If your child sustains an injury and is advised to stop dancing for a period of time, explain to or show the doctor some ballet exercises and determine together whether they are indeed injurious or whether they would facilitate recovery. Physical therapy is usually recommended after an injury, in many instances the ballet class can become part of the rehabilitation process. Talk to the dance teacher, explain the nature of the injury and the recommendation of the doctor, and with that information the teacher can select the types of exercises that the student needs to avoid.

There are two types of injuries: traumatic and chronic. The first is the result of a mishap, like twisting an ankle or pulling a muscle. The second type often follows the first; for example, if a dancer strains the Achilles tendon and does not allow it enough time to heal, he or she may develop tendonitis. A chronic condition such as tendonitis may also develop through habitually incorrect usage of the technique, such as not putting the heels down in jumps (which, again, affects the Achilles tendon).

An injury has three stages, each with its own appropriate care:

Acute: For the first 24 to 48 hours after the injury, no weight should be placed on the injured area; it should be iced, compressed, and elevated.

Sub-acute: After the first 24 to 72 hours, the injured area can be worked carefully to get some motion back, but the patient should not attempt weight-bearing exercises. The area should be alternatively iced and heated. Light massage may be beneficial.

Chronic: If insufficient time is taken for recovery after an injury or the correct treatment has not been followed, a chronic condition may arise. The patient must not overwork the area. Physical therapy and massage are recommended.

Strains

A strain is damage to a tendons or muscle. Strains are basically pulled muscles and vary in severity. Although they can be very painful, the patient should not remain immobile. It is best to gently work through a muscle strain, making sure that the muscle is not overworked and that other parts of the body are not stressed in compensation. However, when a tendon is strained, the severity of the injury determines its treatment. If the tendon is strained at its juncture with the muscle, the condition is less severe than when the tendon is pulled at its insertion into the bone. In this case, greater care in rehabilitation needs to be taken, and immobility may be recommended. In very severe cases surgery is sometimes needed to reattach the tendon.

Inflammation of the tendon is called tendonitis and requires initial rest. The most vulnerable tendon for dancers is the Achilles tendon. However, most dancers work through tendonitis, avoiding motions and positions that cause pain and, when the Achilles tendon is injured, limiting rises on half-pointe and jumps. Icing after a workout is recommended.

Sprains

A sprain is damage to a ligament. They are potentially more serious than strains because ligaments are inelastic. Ligaments stabilize the joints, and because ligaments have a poor supply of blood, the healing process is slow. Sprains are often accompanied by strains because of the damage to surrounding tissues.

Sprains can be caused by misalignment when destabilizing pressure is routinely placed on an area. In this case, the dancer will probably have experienced discomfort for some time and will need to pay attention to the usage of the affected joint. Sprains can also be the result of injury, such as twisting an ankle or knee. Although accidents do occur in dance classes, they are usually the result of improper alignment; therefore, the previous advice still holds true: attention to alignment is the best prevention. As in the case of all injuries, ice should be applied immediately to the affected area. It is usually advisable to see a doctor when a sprain occurs to determine the degree of injury and to make sure no fracture has been sustained. Partial or total immobilization may be recommended for a time; however, the treatment of injuries has changed dramatically over the past fifteen years, and doctors are not as likely as they once were to advise complete immobility or the use of crutches. The doctor may initially advise rest and elevation, and then encourage motions that do not hurt in order to regain mobility of the joint. During rehabilitation, heat and cold should be applied alternatively after working out (twenty minutes for each application). Ice disperses the toxins, heat brings more blood supply to the area, therefore, applying ice, heat then ice again, helps the body repair the injured tissues. Ice and heat used alternatively can also help relieve soreness in muscles: they help to prevent a muscle from going into a chronic "holding pattern." Many dancers routinely ice their muscles before retiring to bed.

Dislocation

Dislocation is not common in dancers. However, should it occur, the intervention of a doctor is necessary to replace the joint. Tissue around the affected joint will have been traumatized, so the rest of the treatment follows the guidelines for sprains and strains. If a child is prone to dislocations, the affected area can be strengthened with physical therapy and special attention to alignment when dancing.

Shinsplints

A shinsplint is a microscopic tearing of ligament fibers in the lower leg away from their point of origin. Like strains and sprains, shinsplints are often caused by misalignment (which includes pronation) or dancing on dance floors that are too hard, and can even be the result of wearing shoes that either are too heavy or have heels of an unusual height. They can even be caused by walking too fast, or by doing too much during a first class after a vacation. The usual treatment for shinsplints is ice and compression, a bandage wrapped around the affected area. If a child complains of shinsplints over an extended period of time, a secondary condition may have arisen; a visit to the doctor and X-rays may be necessary to determine that there are no hairline fractures.

Fractures

Fractures occur in bones. All fractures are severe and require the intervention of a doctor. Only ice should be applied immediately after this type of injury occurs, not heat; heat will only increase inflammation. The area must not be massaged, as this may cause further damage. This is one of the reasons why diagnostic x-rays are important: while massaging may help a strained muscle, it will only cause further damage to a fracture. The length of time that the limb is in a cast will determine the length of the rest period required. Usually a period of rehabilitation is necessary after the cast is removed.

Although a fracture is always serious and may take a long time to heal, it is not fatal to a career. With proper rehabilitation, the dancer can return to her or his craft in time.

Pain-Causing Conditions

A condition common in athletically active girls is the Osgood-Schlatterer's disease, which affects children between the ages of twelve and sixteen. This condition is associated with growth spurts in the tibia and causes pain in the knees. Despite its frightening appellation, Osgood-Schlatterer is a condition that children outgrow. Nevertheless, a child chronically suffering with knee pain should see an orthopedic doctor, preferably one who specializes in sports medicine. The degree of pain experienced and the threshold of pain that the person can withstand will determine how the condition will affect the dancer. Some people anticipate pain while others tend to ignore it; the latter are more successful in working through this condition. I have known students who gave up dancing once this condition was diagnosed, but others have successfully worked through it.

Another common condition is scoliosis, which is a lateral curvature of the spine. Physically active children are often tested for this condition, which varies in severity from a slight curve to one that may affect the alignment of the pelvis. Scoliosis is a common condition; few of us are perfect physical specimens. Dancing can help realign the vertebrae through the tensile strength of the surrounding musculature. If your child has been diagnosed with scoliosis, you should share that information with the teacher, who will then be able to exert extra vigilance in correcting your child's alignment.

Except in extremely severe cases, where physical therapy and a brace are necessary, scoliosis should not be treated as an impairment or an excuse to do less in class. The very nature of ballet training — working both sides of the body equally and in harmony — helps to correct the misalignment that scoliosis creates.

Pain and Compensation

Pain is the body's signal that tissue is damaged. It should not be ignored. On the other hand, because dancers work their bodies with such intensity, some degree of pain is habitually experienced. However, there is a difference between the pain of an overused, tired muscle and one that has been injured. Pain from overuse is usually dull, and will feel better after a hot bath or a gentle massage. An injury is initially accompanied by a sharp pain and often by muscular spasms around the affected area. Because there is no way of knowing immediately the severity of an injury, the steps mentioned earlier are recommended: the area should be iced and elevated, not massaged. Additionally X-rays should be taken to determine the nature and extent of the injury.

The body has wonderful resources that come into play when an injury occurs. One of those resources is called "splinting": the muscles around an injury harden in order to protect from further trauma. Anyone who has been injured has experienced the slow localization of pain: at first a wide area seems to be affected, but as the healing process goes on, the area of pain shrinks to the point of the actual injury. After the injury has been diagnosed and the swelling has gone down, massage and stretching may be prescribed in order to relieve the muscular spasm associated with splinting. Another problem can also arise that dancers need to be acutely aware of after an injury: the body compensates for its inability to fully use the injured area by utilizing other muscles for the same tasks. This compensation may create problems of its own; when a dancer comes back to class after an injury, she or he must be sure to work the body equally without favoring the injured area.

When I was thirteen, I fell onto a spike and gashed out a sizable hole in my left quadricep. Months later I met one of the therapists who had worked with me. He asked me how I was feeling, and I said fine. Then he said "Why are you limping?" I was totally unaware of the compensation that my body had set up and that no longer served any purpose.

Muscle Memory

Dancers rely on muscle memory to perform the increasingly complex motions of the technique, but muscles also retain the memory of trauma, both physical and psychic. A good massage therapist, one that not only knows therapy but has worked with dancers, can work these "memories" out of the system.

I like to think of the body as an engine. The body of a dancer is a very sophisticated instrument, like a Rolls-Royce engine. Maintenance of such an engine must also be sophisticated. Therefore, when seeking medical help you must find the people who have the most experience with soft tissues, muscles, and bones. Sports doctors who are knowledgeable about dance, orthopedic doctors, osteopaths, chiropractors, physical therapists, and acupuncturists have the expertise necessary to help diagnose problems and prescribe correct treatments. Applied kinesiologists and massage therapists are especially sensitive to the problems of dancers and can provide the care needed for complete rehabilitation.

HELPING THE BODY TO RECOVER

To help the body recover, the patient should avoid neural stimulants. Substances containing caffeine are definitely off-limits; the complete list includes coffee, tea, chocolate, soft drinks containing caffeine or NutraSweet, and all products containing mint. The chemicals often found in food additives end up being stored in the muscles and affect their ability to repair and renew. Water flushes out the impurities in the system and help the body heal itself. Breathing deeply brings needed oxygen, which also plays a part in the healing process. I know from experience that it is hard to stop the panic after you have sustained an injury, but panic and fear also interfere with healing.

A balanced diet, a regimen of breathing exercises (such as that which yoga techniques provide), enough rest and sleep, and attention to alignment in dance classes will go a long way in preventing injuries. But should an injury occur, it must be remembered that the doctor is not a magician; he or she needs the patient's cooperation if the healing is to be successful. Furthermore, suffering from aches and pains has to be accepted as a part of dance discipline. When the muscles are constantly stretched and flexed, a certain amount of lactic acid builds up and causes temporary stiffness and a mild ache. This is not a sign of injury, but one of intense use; the cure is to go on dancing in class. As the body warms up, the aches disappear. It is only when the pain persists that there is reason to be concerned about a possible problem. If repeated injuries are sustained or a chronic condition has developed, such as tendonitis or bursitis, the execution of the technique may be at fault. Reexamining (with the aid of a professional) the understanding of the technique and analyzing alignment and the way specific motions are performed are the solutions to the problem. The Fieldenkrais, Alexander, and Pilates techniques provide that sort of analysis and recondition the body for an efficient use of the musculature.

As young professional students at the Paris Opera School, we were forbidden to engage in any athletic activity. Ice-skating, horseback riding, and even team sports like volleyball were off-limits. The reason given for this edict was that sports build muscles that are not desirable for dancers and, additionally, expose you to the risk of injury. When a child becomes serious about dance and considers it as a career, she or he should avoid sports. A strained knee or ankle is a momentary impediment to most people, but for dancers it becomes a serious setback.

Make sure that your studio has some ice and some leakproof baggies, or a supply of ice packs, and some Ace bandages. If the child is on pointe, she should carry some moleskin in her dance bag. Prevention is always the best policy. A balanced diet, enough rest, working with an aligned body, and avoiding activities that are inherently risky should ensure an injury-free experience in dance.

Two excellent books on dance-related injuries cover this subject in more depth: *Preventing Dance Injuries,* edited by Ruth Solomon, Sandra C. Minton, and John Solomon (American Alliance for Health, Physical Education, Recreation and Dance, 1990); and the *Dancer's Guide to Injuries of the Lower Extremities,* by Stuart Wright (Cornwall Books, 1985). The first uses rather technical language but discusses the whole body, while the second is more accessible to the lay reader but only addresses, as its title suggests, the lower extremities.

Students of the Chicago Academy for the Arts.
©1997 Mitchell Canoff

❧ 9 ❧

Diet and Eating Disorders

WE LIVE in a diet-conscious age and are subjected, on an almost daily basis, to new discoveries of the properties of food. We know a great deal about nutrition, especially which foods to avoid, and we appreciate the connection between nutrition and health. Nevertheless, as a nation we persist in all sorts of destructive eating habits.

Just as we go overboard in our indulgences, so we can also become fanatical about our diets. As the parent of a young dancer, you must be aware of the types of stress that are associated with the profession: the emphasis on thinness; the concern with and acute awareness of the shape of the body; and, too often, a disparaging attitude toward achievements. These stresses sometimes contribute to push an otherwise healthy child into experimenting with food. However, you must also be aware that for your dancing child, eating less than siblings is normal because the dancer is more concerned with the body. Awareness is, in many ways, a survival tactic. To succeed in the dance world, a dancer has to maintain an optimum weight. This awareness also makes dancers more prone to all sorts of extremes in their diets.

While being overweight is not healthy, an obsession with thinness may be even worse. Young dancers model themselves on mature artists without realizing that the streamlining depends on age and training as much as it does on the right diet. If we do not obtain the proper nourishment during the growing years, we may stunt our growth and affect our level of energy. This type of willful malnutrition may have serious physical and medical repercussions in later years.

The best advice I have heard on this topic came from a doctor after the birth of my first child. He said, "Eat everything in small amounts, never have seconds, avoid sweets, and never eat between meals." Within three months, I was back to the weight I had been before the pregnancy, and the extra weight stayed off.

Awareness of what and how much is good for us is the first step toward a balanced diet. The percentages of daily dietary need (established by the American Heart Association, the National Academy of Sciences, and the National Institutes of Health) are 55 percent carbohydrates, 15 percent protein, and 30 percent fat. Recent studies suggest that especially for physically active people and growing children, this percentage of carbohydrates may be excessive; more protein in the diet would be beneficial. The ideal ratio in this case would be 30 percent carbohydrates, 40 percent protein, and 30 percent fat.

DIETARY ELEMENTS
Carbohydrates

Complex carbohydrates are composed of sugars, starches, minerals, vitamins, and some protein. Broken down by our digestive system, they provide the fuel we need. Complex carbohydrates include potatoes, pasta, bread, rice, corn, and a variety of vegetables and legumes.

Protein

Protein has long been considered the major source of energy; it feeds our muscles. Complete protein products include all meats and dairy foods; however, dairy foods such as cheese have a higher percentage of fat than most meats.

Fat

A misapprehension of the function of fat has led some people to eliminate it almost entirely from their diet. Fat is a necessary dietary component, ensuring healthy skin and hair and aiding in the absorption of fat-soluble vitamins, such as A, D, E, and K.

Fiber

Although fiber has no nutritional value, it is a necessary component of any diet because it aids digestion. Fiber can be found in most vegetables and unrefined grains.

It must be remembered that our dietary needs change as we grow older. A growing child who is building bones needs more protein than an adult. Additionally, dancers need more protein than less active people to help muscles repair and rebuild. But it is also a fact that dance is not an aerobic activity, and dancers do not burn as many calories as do athletes who are engaged in an aerobic activity. (Some studios encourage and sometimes provide an aerobic program for their students.) If a person's metabolic rate is slow, dancing will not change it; she or he has either to engage in an activity, such as walking, that will speed metabolism, or to limit food intake.

A balanced diet that will provide between 1200 and 1500 calories includes:

Carbohydrates: 4 portions. One portion equals one slice of bread (preferably whole-wheat), one cup of dry cereal, one cup of pasta or rice, or one small baked potato.

Vegetables and fruit: 4 portions. One portion equals one piece of fruit or 1 cup of raw or cooked vegetables.

Lactose: 2 portions for adults, 4 portions for adolescents. One portion equals eight ounces of milk, eight ounces of low-fat yogurt, one ounce of cheese, or one cup of cottage cheese.

Protein: 2 portions. One portion equals four ounces of meat, poultry, or fish, or one cup of beans.

Adapted from Allan J. Ryan, M.D., and Robert E. Stephens, Ph.D., *The Healthy Dancer.* NJ: Princeton Book Company, 1987, p. 85.)

A typical day with a diet of this kind may look like this:

Breakfast: a bowl of cereal with eight ounces of low-fat milk, a piece of fruit, and a piece of whole-wheat toast or a muffin.

Lunch: a small salad or a bowl of soup, a turkey or tuna-fish sandwich, and a piece of fruit.

Snack: a choice of two items: carrot sticks, a piece of fruit, raisins, yogurt, a couple of whole-wheat cookies or crackers.

Dinner: meat (a small steak, chicken breast or thigh, or fish filet); pasta or potatoes; green beans, spinach, or zucchini; a small green salad; and bread.

A diet that includes more protein would allow more meat, fish, or poultry and less bread, pasta products, potatoes, and corn (corn is extremely high in sugar content and should generally be avoided). This type of diet would increase the protein intake to 3 portions and reduce the carbohydrates and vegetables/fruit to 2 portions each.

Here are a few ideas to remember in maintaining or regaining control over what and how much to eat:

1. Establish a regimen of three or four meals a day, eaten at approximately the same time every day.

2. How much you eat is as significant as what you eat. Never have seconds. (Do not cheat by piling food on the plate in anticipation of not being allowed seconds.)

3. Have a variety of foods every day.

4. Love what you eat. Pay attention while eating every item on the plate.

5. Listen to your needs. Sometimes a craving for a particular food indicates a deficiency of a particular vitamin or mineral. (Candy bars are excluded!)

6. Do not eat between meals. Do not eat snack foods such as potato chips, cookies, manufactured snacks, etc.

7. Do not add sugar to tea or coffee.

8. Learn the difference between hunger and turning to food because you are bored or upset.

9. If you must snack, make it fruit or yogurt; both will provide more lasting energy than a candy bar.

10. Avoid food with preservatives.

A couple of years ago, I took a survey of the diets of the dancers at my school. For one week they kept a record of everything they ate. Only a few had regular meals with their families. The majority ate sandwiches and fast food takeouts; one of them lived almost entirely on Twinkies. Talking with the students about balanced diets helped them become aware of the impact that an adequate regimen has on their energy level, ability to concentrate, and general well-being. They now consume far fewer candy bars and more fruit and vegetables between classes.

Sitting down to a meal, no matter how modest, is a ritual that transcends the mere intake of food for survival. Breaking bread with those you love is an acknowledgment and celebration of the bonds that unite you. Preparation of that food, which need not be elaborate, is very much part of that ritual. Eating assumes a rightful place in the rhythm of life, and food nourishes the soul as well as sustains the body.

EATING DISORDERS

In talking about dancers, we cannot avoid the subject of eating disorders. Although dancers are not the only people who suffer from eating disorders, they are particularly susceptible because the milieu in which they work demands and rewards thinness, and because their character profile closely matches the general profile of people who are prone to this condition.

Dancers live and work in a highly autocratic milieu. They learn through being criticized, with little if any positive reinforcement of their talent. The result is not only a poor self-image but an overreliance on the opinion of the mentor. Dancers may not trust their own perceptions, and thus tend to develop a warped self-image; seeing fat where there are only bones is only one aspect of this. Every morning dancers face their image in the mirror, and every motion, every line of the body comes under scrutiny, both their own and the teacher's. They pass judgment, a judgment that has been formed by looking at their fellow dancers and an often unrealistic, imagined ideal. (For a thoroughly enlightening discussing of this subject, see Dr. L. M. Vincent's *Competing with the Sylph.*

In her book *Dancing on My Grave,* Gelsey Kirkland, former balle-rina with the New York City Ballet and American Ballet Theatre, says:

> Mr. Balanchine's ideal proportions called for an almost skeletal frame, ac-centuating the collarbones and length of the neck. Defeminization was the overall result, with frequent cessation of the menstrual cycle due to mal-nutrition and physical abuse. . . . Many of the excesses of American ballet seem to be the result of the slimness trend, turning the ideal of beauty into mere fashion. Mr. B pushed us in that direction, but he also popularized ballet. This offers the hope that the public may press for reform — as an increasing number of ballet parents become concerned for the welfare of their children. (p 56.).

Some doctors believe that some people may have a genetic and or physiological predisposition to eating disorders. The psychological profile seems to play a central role: typically, anorexics are perfection-ists — meticulous, scholarly, and compliant. These same qualities are shared by many dancers who continually strive to please mentors or parents and, in the process, fail to develop their own individuality.

A low level of self-esteem and a distorted perception of physical appearance are, according to psychiatrists, only the tip of the iceberg. Some people are medically and/or socially predisposed to slip into an-orexia. Slipping into the condition may be a very apt way of describ-ing its onset. The disorder actually begins with an obsession with food. As one dancer describes it: "I read about food; I dreamed about food; I thought about food. I knew the exact caloric content of every type of food. I had set my limit at 1000 calories. A slice of bread and cheese amounted to 300 calories, I would say 'I can't have that, it will put me over my limit'." She subsisted on a salad for lunch and a bowl of popcorn for dinner. Her energy level dropped and she stopped menstruating, yet every time she looked in the mirror she saw her im-perfections and felt that her only recourse was to lose more weight.

Dancers are not the only people who suffer from eating disorders. We need only look around us to see the large number of overweight people in this country. The opposite extreme is less detectable because we admire thinness in our culture, pursue it with diets and exercise, and compliment each other when we lose a few pounds. Although eat-ing disorders often affect girls in their prepubescent and adolescent years, they are not limited to that age group and can claim victims of both sexes and all ages; however, 90 percent of people suffering from anorexia and bulimia are women. The onset of these disorders typically occurs between the ages of twelve and eighteen but can occur later. Anorexia and bulimia are characterized by an obsessive fear of being fat, bolstered by an unrealistic self-image; individuals perceive themselves as fat when they are in fact normal or even underweight.

Talking with dancers about weight elicits many similar stories. We have all stood in front of the mirror in the dressing room and pointed to our hips or buttocks, seeing the piece of chocolate consumed in a weak moment the previous night. Most of us have experimented with crazy diets in which black coffee and carrots, grapefruit, or milk and bananas provide the only sustenance for days. Some of us have even taken laxatives in the belief that the food we consumed would move through our systems much faster and therefore would not turn to fat. Fortunately, most of us have outgrown these adolescent obsessions and do not have a chronic weight problem, although we go on watching what and how much we eat.

Between the ages of fourteen and twenty, the body begins to fill out as the girl becomes a woman. Unfortunately, this period also corresponds to a period of intense training and, for some, entrance into the professional world. Therefore, the onset of womanhood is sometimes perceived not as a natural evolution but as a threat. This is further complicated in the ballet world by the notion that an ideal figure for a ballerina should be extremely thin and sylphlike. Balanchine championed a group of so-called "baby ballerinas" in the thirties and forties whose pre-adolescent body types became the norm for many performers. Thus, a young girl who is developing a "figure" may starve herself to maintain her prepubescent look.

Anorexics starve themselves; they eat small portions of food or sometimes stop eating altogether. Their bodies do not receive enough nourishment to sustain normal functions. The menstrual cycle is interrupted, because it depends upon a certain percentage of fat in the body to function properly. The normal percentage of body fat is between 20 and 25 percent of total weight; dancers tend to carry no more than 13 to 18 percent. When the percentage of fat falls below 12 percent, the menstrual cycle is interrupted. If anorexia is not checked, the body begins to consume itself.

Bulimics indulge in binge eating and purging as a means of controlling their weight. The purging may take the form of induced vomiting, diuretics, or diet pills and laxatives. Extreme damage to teeth, caused by stomach acids, is among the many physical side effects of bulimia.

The National Association of Anorexia Nervosa and Associated Disorders (ANAD), whose headquarters are in Chicago, warns that "early detection and intervention are critical in saving lives. Because many anorexics and bulimics deny that they are ill, family and friends play a critical role in recognizing eating disorder problems and getting help immediately. Although not all victims display all symptoms, several danger signals are commonly associated with anorexia and bulimia."

Symptoms of anorexia nervosa outlined by ANAD:

Deliberate self-starvation with weight loss

Intense, persistent fear of gaining weight

Refusal to eat

Continuous dieting

Denial of hunger

Compulsive exercise

Excessive facial/body hair

Distorted body image

Abnormal weight loss

Sensitivity to cold

Absent or irregular menstruation

Hair loss

Symptoms of bulimia nervosa outlined by ANAD:

Preoccupation with food

Binge eating, usually in secret

Vomiting after bingeing

Abuse of laxatives, diuretics, diet pills or emetics

Compulsive exercising
Swollen salivary glands
Broken blood vessels in eyes

Telling an anorexic that she is too thin is futile. Dr. Alexander Golbin, a Chicago pediatrician and psychiatrist, says that the anorexic has no sense of the disease. Dr. Golbin does not confront his patients, but rather works around their reluctance until they are able to face the facts. However, most sufferers agree that anorexia is not simply a habit; it is part of them. Although they may return to a more healthful relationship with food and a more realistic self-image, preoccupation with weight and food may never truly leave them.

Early intervention is essential in breaking the self-destructive cycle. If your child exhibits even one of the symptoms listed above, accompanied by a 10-percent weight loss, treatment should be sought immediately. Once she has developed an obsession with thinness, there is no other recourse, according to Dr. Golbin.

Even in the pre-professional dance world, your child will be exposed to extreme opinions about weight management. A realistic self-image, a healthy attitude toward food, and a supportive and loving environment will go a long way in preventing obsessive behavior.

Students of the Chicago Academy for the Arts.
©1997 Mitchell Canoff

✳ 10 ✳

Entering the Profession

T HE GREATEST difference among dance companies is size, not idiom. Large companies will be administered in similar ways, be they modern dance, jazz, or ballet. Furthermore, as mentioned earlier, today there are very few companies that do not have a mixed repertory. The large company may have an extended touring schedule, although regional companies, such as the Houston Ballet or the Louisville Ballet, tend to cultivate their hometown audiences.

Medium-sized companies, especially modern-dance groups, may supplement their performing schedule with an outreach program, offering lecture/demonstrations in public schools. Both large and medium-sized companies generally offer a contract for between twenty-two weeks and a full year. Additionally, they often have associated schools that employ their dancers as teachers.

Small companies and "pickup" groups engage dancers for a specific series of performances. They seldom offer contracts; dancers may get paid per performance. But they form the grass roots from which bigger endeavors may spring.

AUDITIONS

By the time students are ready to audition for their first professional engagement, they will have had, in all likelihood, some experience with the process through an audition for a summer program or a special performance. Whether seeking admission to a university program or membership in a dance company, dancers must always audition, which generally means that the prospective members take a class.

Auditionees should come fully prepared to dance and have all that they need to make a neat and efficient impression, such as a plain leotard and tights, shoes that have been broken in, enough hairpins to keep the hair in place, and a couple of safety pins in case a ribbon or strap comes loose. Parachute pants or bulky legwarmers should never be worn at an audition.

If the audition starts with barre work, the dancer should select a place where s/he will be comfortable. It is best not to stand in corners if the audition is crowded; otherwise legs may get tangled with the person standing at the right angle. Coming into the center, the dancer should not hang back, but should step to the front of the class. This action will show the selectors self-confidence, and will also enable them to see the auditionee clearly. Additionally, it will provide the auditionee with a better view of the teacher demonstrating the combination. If the class is divided into groups, the dancer should not wait for the last group to step forward. By joining the first or second group, the dancer demonstrates that she or he is a quick learner. Similarly, when combinations are given from the corner on a diagonal, the dancer should join one of the first groups going across the floor. It is best to avoid asking questions like "Which arm is up?" or "Do we start with the right leg back?" Instead, the dancer should look closely at all the details demonstrated by the teacher, marking the combination so that it is firmly set in the body. Being aware of the demonstrator's style is especially important in jazz and modern-dance auditions; the auditioner will be looking at adaptability.

Some companies request that the dancer supply a resume and photograph at the time of the audition. The fact that the dancer may not have a lot of professional experience should not prove a hindrance. Companies are generally more interested in the kind of training that the dancers have received, their current level of proficiency, and their ability to pick up combinations. I was once engaged for a film almost solely on the strength of having studied with Olga Preobrazhenskaya. Before we were asked to dance, the director wanted to know where we had studied, and she retained only the people that she felt had received correct training.

There are many different kinds of auditions, each with its own format. If the audition is for a specific production, like *The Nutcracker*, for which the company simply needs to supplement its roster of dancers, the auditioners will probably be looking for dancers to fill specific parts. If, on the other hand, the audition is held to engage contract dancers for an entire season, the director may be looking for someone to fit into the current repertory. Some companies favor tall dancers; others prefer shorter ones. Some like dancers of a normal weight; others accept only bone-thin dancers. It is wise to inquire, before making a trip to a distant city, what kind of physique the company favors. Modern companies tend to be less picky about the physique and engage dancers on the strength of their technique, style, and personality.

Competition is fierce in the dance world, especially for female dancers. There are just too many aspiring ballerinas and not enough good companies to provide employment for all of them. Once a student has been accepted into a company, the competition for advancement is largely a matter of talent and personality. The lucky dancers find their choreographer, or the choreographer finds his or her interpreter. There have been some notable partnerships of this kind. Choreographer Frederick Ashton (1904–1988) had dancer Margot Fonteyn (1919–1991); John Cranko (1927–1973) had Marcia Haydee (b. 1937); Kenneth Macmillan (b. 1929) had Lynn Seymour (b. 1939); and George Balanchine featured a different ballerina in each of the phases of his creative life. Of course, these dancers form an elite circle open to few; countless successful dancers have not found this kind of public recognition but have nevertheless had fulfilling careers.

Despite the competitiveness of the dance world, dancers as a group tend to be supportive of each other. They form within any one company a close community with common goals and common complaints. Because dancers work such long hours, they have little opportunity to form friendships outside the group. This is especially true of companies that have a busy touring schedule. Often dancers do not even know which city they are visiting, unless they have a few free hours during the day and the hosts make a special effort to allow for some sightseeing expeditions. This closeness also breeds a certain exclusivity, whereupon new members may not be welcomed into the inner circle immediately and may find their first weeks in a company somewhat solitary. Perhaps this attitude is no different from that of other workplaces, but it is simply magnified here because the dance company is such a closed environment. Its members forced to rely on each other to a degree that outsiders find difficult to understand or appreciate.

FINDING WORK

A young dancer can obtain her or his first engagement in various ways. The services of an agent are not necessary unless the dancer seeks commercial work, such as television, films, or industrials (shows that cater to conventions). Most Broadway-type shows hold open auditions, sometimes termed "cattle calls" because they attract so many applicants. These auditions are generally advertised in the trade magazines. Many regional ballet companies also advertize their needs and audition dates in *Dance* Magazine, among other dance publications. Established modern-dance and jazz companies usually hold internal auditions for their roster of apprentices. Auditions are usually held in the spring for the following season beginning in September. However, a company will seldom turn away a prospective member if she or he happens to be in town and contacts the organization; the dancer will be invited to take a class, and if there are no immediate vacancies, the dancer will at least be known the next time she or he auditions. Some companies even have a policy of open classes, through which people who are not in the company can take class with company members. Each company is bound to have its own guidelines, and it is a good idea to check them before embarking on a tour of prospects.

Besides the cold-audition route, many dancers find work through personal recommendation. The home teacher may have some contacts, or a visiting guest teacher may be willing to write a recommendation or suggest a venue. Attending a summer workshop may result in an invitation to join the associated company or become an apprentice. An apprenticeship is not a guarantee of acceptance into the company, but it is one step closer.

Some organizations like to imbue the dancers with their particular style, so they insist that dancers undergo a period of apprenticeship or attend their associated school prior to being considered for the company. When auditioning for a first professional engagement, the dancer will, in most cases, be engaged initially as an apprentice. The more prestigious the company, the greater choice of dancers the company has, and therefore the more restrictions they place on prospective members.

Like many professions, the dance field is all too easily exploitive. Dancers are often viewed as a commodity — if the dancer does not fulfill the initial promise, a dozen others are waiting in the wings. Dancers need to be aware that they are easily replaceable; but they must also watch for situations that may endanger their health, such as a punishing rehearsal schedule, lack of regular technique classes, or a high turnover rate. They need to remember that being accepted into a particular company is only the beginning. They must not only maintain their technique but improve it if they want to qualify for better roles; and, above all, their first allegiance must be to their own growth and well-being.

In most large companies, the dancers belong to the American Guild of Musical Artists (AGMA). A union contract specifies how many hours dancers are expected to rehearse on non-performance as well as performance days. On a normal day, one without a performance, dancers can rehearse for up to five hours; this, of course, is in addition to a company class. On a performance day, dancers may only rehearse for two hours. When they are performing twice in a single day, they may not rehearse at all. When on tour, they may travel for seven hours on non-performance days but for only four on performance days. Dancers must have a two-hour break after their arrival in town. They may rehearse for up to three hours the day of opening night.

The union contract also specifies wages. The national standard for a first-year dancer's salary is $500 per week. The salary rises each year but is also dependent on the artist's ranking and, eventually, seniority. A soloist may get $1,600 per week or more, depending on her or his standing within the company. We must bear in mind that the contract may not be for a year but for a specified number of weeks, as few as twenty-two weeks in some instances. During the layoff period, dancers may accept engagements with other companies, teach, or go on unemployment.

At the other end of the scale are countless small, non-union companies that may pay as little as $200 a week or pay the dancers on a per-performance basis. If there is a contract, it usually covers a relatively short span of time. Dancers employed by these small companies usually have to supplement their incomes with part-time jobs.

TOURING

A professional dancer must be prepared to work when others rest (evenings and holidays) as well as when others work (morning classes, afternoon rehearsals, or daytime performances). A dancer will also be away from home a great deal. Few dance companies can survive by performing solely in their home city, so touring is an integral part of the season.

Touring may be anything from short day or overnight trips to weeks on the road. Generally, the sole responsibility of dancers is to be at the departure point on time; travel and accommodations are arranged by the company. Some companies turn over to the dancers the frequent-flyer mileage accumulated during the tour, which sometimes provides for a vacation trip during the off-season. However, the dancers are responsible for their personal effects and for taking care of their laundry needs. Sometimes they even have to wash their own costumes, and are then given extra money to cover the cost. While on tour, dancers receive a per-diem allowance that ranges from $40 to $60. The allowance varies according to the cost of living in the country visited. Some companies give a higher allowance when the hotel bill is the responsibility of the dancer.

Eating on tour may present a challenge. Many smaller cities do not have restaurants that stay open late at night, and finding a place to eat after the performance may be a problem. Winifred Haun, a member of Joseph Holmes Chicago Dance Theatre for eight years, says that people tend to either lose or gain weight during the touring season. Often the only available food is from fast-food restaurants, and finding the type of food you usually eat is difficult. She adds, however, that sometimes presenters will provide refreshments after a performance; "small amenities really make us happy." Patty Eylar, a member of the Chicago Ballet, says that it is too easy to get out of shape on tour: "We have classes on performance days, but not on the days when we are traveling. It is hard to find studios that will give you a space for class. The stage manager finds restaurants for us or picks up sandwiches for the company. We do laundry on our day off. It's hard." She speaks of touring in Europe as having been especially difficult: "Every time we wanted to eat, the stores were closed. Everyone was taking a nap!" On one occasion, traveling from France to Italy, the road was closed, the bus had to take a detour, and the dancers ended up being on the road for twenty-one hours. But "we saw some wonderful scenery."

While the novelty of touring may be exciting at the beginning, dancers soon miss their habitual surroundings. Haun says, "You find that you are thrown in the company of people that you would not generally have much in common with. You soon know who your real friends are." Whenever we find ourselves in new surroundings with irregular routines, we tend to lose the anchoring that a regular routine provides. To maintain healthy eating habits, a degree of technique, and a sense of humor takes a lot of discipline.

A life in dance demands extraordinary commitment. Dancers work long hours at a physically exhausting task. They need to keep their instrument (the body) in peak condition, which does not allow for many self-indulgences. As Ivan Nagy commented on the disparity of the perceived glamour of the profession and its reality, "You do a plié in New York, or London, or Moscow, and it still hurts." Dancers lead, for the most part, an existence that is somewhat isolated from the mainstream — often the busiest season for a company is vacation time for the rest of society. For most dancers, dance is not what they do but who they are. Dancing could be likened to climbing a mountain. As you take each step, you exult in your ability to do so, your muscles hurt, your hands (or feet) bleed, you labor to reach the next plateau, and, looking upward, you see how far you have yet to scale. And there is joy in looking at the road yet to be traveled, because the joy is in the doing.

With all the hardships that a life in dance implies, dancers are extremely lucky people; they are engaged in doing what they love. The discipline of dance provides transcendal moments on a daily basis. Our culture is given to finding "last frontiers" to fuel the imagination: the West, Alaska, outer space. Dancers are actively engaged in conquering their frontier every day; aching muscles and less-than-ideal working conditions are a small price to pay for the privilege.

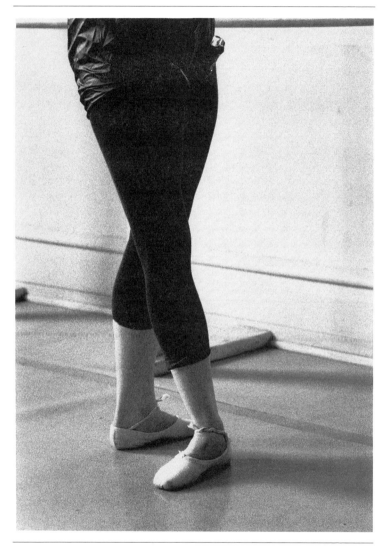

Student of the Chicago Academy for the Arts.
©1997 Mitchell Canoff

Beyond Secondary Education
and a Dancing Career

A COMMONLY held belief in dance is that younger is not only better: it is essential. According to some dance professionals, if one is intent on a dance career, the years spent attending college are dangerously detracting. Many young dancers feel compelled to enter professional dance schools or apprenticeship within a company often without even having finished high school. Some professionals hold that those who have not achieved the status of soloist by the age of twenty-one or twenty-two will, in all probability, never rise beyond the ranks of the corps de ballet. In order to become a soloist, one must be dancing professionally by the age of eighteen at the latest. In other words, all energies, leading up to acceptance into a company, must be directed toward dancing; there can be no question of a college education interrupting the momentum. While the late teens are unquestionably essential formative years during which young dancers must be engaged in honing their skills, this denies a young dancer the chance to enjoy other, "normal" teenage experiences and ignores the many alternatives that are available for continuing an education. These alternatives include enrolling as a part-time student in a university while engaged in a professional company.

The above model for a dancing career is based on the European and Russian ballet schools, where children enter a professional school at the age of nine or ten and are educated within the institution. Alexandre Demidov writes, in his *Russian Ballet Past and Present,* "The training in ballet schools is aimed not only at developing professional skills but at fostering the general cultural growth of the students who have chosen the hard work of a dancer. . . . The curricula of these schools are such that the future ballet dancer will be a broadly educated person, a cultured person in the highest sense of that word" (p. 13). As this statement indicates, the general education of these dancers is not sacrificed to dance. On the contrary, dancers receive a broad, liberal-arts education prior to their entry into the professional world; an education, moreover, that bears more resemblance to an undergraduate college program than it does to the standards of most American high schools.

In this country, while we have adopted the view that dancers need to be engaged in their profession at an early age, we overlook the general education that the Russian and European models embrace. This narrowness of focus often results in dancers who, while achieving high standards in the art form, have nevertheless been denied the opportunity to mature intellectually and emotionally.

The urgency to start early in a professional career is in part based on the fact that the performing life within dance is comparatively short. By age thirty-five, if not sooner, dancers begin to think of alternate ways to make a living. Furthermore, the risk of injury is always present. The emotional impact of an injury is compounded by the fear that you may be overlooked for roles. Claire Bataille, of Chicago's Hubbard Street Dance Theatre, comments, "You dance when injured because you are afraid they may forget about you." Of course, the greatest fear of all is that of not being able to dance anymore. But what kind of choices does, for example, a twenty-nine-year-old dancer have, when she or he does not even have a high-school diploma and has never done anything but dance since the age of eight? The very brevity of this career supports the argument for a college education.

One of the purposes of education is surely to provide choices. A dancer's education is often lopsided. Concentrating from an early age on this physically demanding activity may lead to neglecting other aspects of development. Higher education opens up opportunities unimaginable to a fourteen-year-old whose horizons are bounded by the ballet studio. The four years spent at a college or university may prove the very stepping-stone one needs for a successful and rewarding career. Not only will they provide the benefits of the intellectual pursuits that are the fabric of education, but they also may open doors to the professional dance world through the friendships formed and the artists met. The experience of a college education may also, later on, facilitate the transition from a dancing career. It may suggest exciting choices and help the dancer assess her or his strengths and interests.

COLLEGE DANCE PROGRAMS

Modern dance led the way for dance to become a discipline that could be taught at the college level. Bennington College held its first summer dance course in 1934 and became the mecca for many dancers who wanted to work with the modern-dance pioneers — people like Martha Graham, Hanya Holm, Doris Humphrey, and Charles Weidman. After the war, university dance programs proliferated, but ballet was not incorporated into the curriculum on any appreciable scale until the late 1960s. Today over five hundred colleges offer a dance curriculum and degree. Ballet and modern dance are usually, but not always, taught side-by-side within the same program.

While one university program seems much the same as another on the surface, dancers need to look deeper to determine a program's particular strengths in order to match them to their own predominant interests. In a college program, students can expect to learn, besides general-education subjects, kinesiology, dance history, and the basic principles of choreography. Some programs also offer dance criticism, aesthetics, and teacher training.

Most dance programs have an active performing schedule, but again they vary greatly in both content and quality depending on the interests and backgrounds of the faculty. In some departments modern dance is emphasized, while in others ballet predominates. Some colleges even have affiliations with the local ballet or modern-dance company, providing a further outlet for the students to gain performance experience.

The knowledge gained during a four-year undergraduate program enhances the physical experience of dance and enables the dancer to develop into a knowledgeable teacher or choreographer. Far from being a detraction, those years allow the individual to grow, form opinions, and develop into an artist with a full grasp of the chosen art form. Additional benefits of a college education are the contacts that students make through the resident faculty and visiting artists. These contacts provide entry both into the professional world and into teaching or choreography. Additionally, the undergraduate degree makes the transition to another career easier when the performing years are over.

Moreover, while most modern-dance companies unquestionably prefer their dancers to have reached a certain level of maturity, many ballet companies are also turning to more mature dancers. They appreciate the deeper understanding of motion and emotion that seasoned performers bring to the repertory. Therefore, the notion that younger is better is usually not borne out through experience.

Every year *Dance* Magazine publishes a comprehensive guide to universities and colleges. Additionally, many universities hold national auditions and advertise the dates and locations in this popular magazine. A dance student who wishes to enter a college dance program should initiate some investigation a year or two ahead of the entry year. This time will allow for some visits and observations that will help in the selection of a program best suited to the student's talents and interests.

BEYOND A PERFORMING CAREER

Many dance-related careers are open to dancers. Some require an undergraduate college degree, while others may require either further college education or on-the-job-training.

Teaching

The most obvious career choice for continuing a direct association with dance is teaching. The only real requirement for teaching at a studio is a thorough knowledge of the art form.

While a college degree is not required to open a dance studio, a knowledge of business will help the studio be financially successful.

Dance teachers face landlords and leases and must keep accurate records, balance expenses against income, and pay taxes. They must also know how to advertise their program and how to devise a curriculum.

Unless the school will be in a town where there are no other dance schools, teachers need to survey the competition to determine how their proposed program differs from the others and how it will enhance the dance education in that area. This survey will initially help in targeting prospective students and designing an advertising campaign to reach them.

When I opened my first school in New Jersey in 1966, I devised an inexpensive campaign. We printed flyers, and my children and I spent a week stuffing mailboxes within a ten-mile radius of the studio. Then I placed an ad in the local newspaper a month prior to the start of school in September, to remind those I had already contacted and to reach others outside the ten-mile radius. Even this primitive form of advertising brought enough students to open the school. The best kind of publicity for a new school, however, is a story with pictures in a local newspaper. It gives a teacher the opportunity to describe her or his approach and background, and the coverage greatly facilitates recruitment.

Devising a curriculum requires knowledge of the developmental aspects of the technique — what is appropriate at various levels and for specific age groups, from creative movement to advanced levels. Neophyte teachers need not rely on their training experience alone to guide them; teacher-training courses at a local college are invaluable. Working with a mentor who is knowledgeable about the developmental aspects of dance training is another option. There are also numerous books on the subject of teaching dance.

If the studio owner does not teach all the classes, there must be a basis for evaluating the competence of those who teach. The same concerns that guide one's own teaching apply to employees — are the material and the pace of the class appropriate? Are the corrections given to students based upon sound principles? Can the teacher demonstrate the motions with competence? The employer may even have to train teachers to conform to her or his ideals.

Rather than assuming the responsibility of opening their own studio, many dancers choose the path of a freelance teacher. Dancers who move on to a freelance teaching career generally choose to remain in the city where they are known through their work with the local dance company. The first step is contacting the local dance schools to make them aware of one's availability. The chief requirement is adaptability; each studio will have its own code of conduct and expectations, and a freelance teacher will have to conform to them.

There are other issues to consider when planning a freelance teaching career. A freelance dance teacher is paid by the class, so one will need to line up enough classes, often in different studios, to make a decent living. The very real drawback to freelancing is the fact that studios generally do not offer health plans or benefits, and there is absolutely no job security: the contracts are often verbal, and classes may be canceled with little notice.

While many university dance programs are headed by former dancers without degrees, these dancers have usually held prominent places in the dance world prior to their retirement into teaching. These same universities require at least a master's degree of their prospective teachers if they have not achieved preeminent status in the professional world. Although many colleges employ dancers without degrees in junior-faculty positions, the dancer must hold a master's degree to be eligible for tenure-track positions.

Adjunct faculty depend upon yearly contracts and, like freelance teachers, have no benefits. Salaries for adjuncts are usually quite low, so adjuncts often find it necessary to supplement income by teaching at other places. With a bachelor's degree, reentry and completion of a master's degree in a university graduate program is usually fairly straightforward. Even if not, the prospect of several years spent obtaining these two degrees should not be daunting. Colleges often give credit for life experience and for competency in one's field.

Teaching dance at public high schools is also an option. However, state certification is generally required for eligibility. Different states have different criteria; some require certification prior to employment, while others allow the dance teacher to obtain certification while teaching.

Choreography

It has been said that choreographers are not made but born, that dancers cannot learn choreography but must be blessed with some innate talent. There are, however, many levels of choreographic endeavors. All teachers are choreographers, because designing a class involves combining steps in interesting ways. Composing for a class, however, differs from composing a ballet. A teacher is bound by the rules of the technique, whereas choreographers, like poets, can break academic rules to achieve desired effects. Choreographers need a sense of composition (an eye for patterns and balance in space); musicality (an ear not only for the rhythmic patterns but also for the emotional content of a musical composition); an ability to abstract feelings and translate them into motion; and the ability to tell a story using motion instead of words. Working with young children also requires adaptability, a tempering of what one imagines to the technical and emotional level of the students.

These qualities can be developed through association with and participation in the repertory of a company. Great choreographers of the past, such as Marius Petipa, Mikhail Fokine, Frederick Ashton, Antony Tudor, and George Balanchine learned the craft of choreography in this manner. Not only did they have a strong desire to create dances, but they were given the opportunity to refine their craft over a long period of time. They learned through trial and error; they experienced failures as well as outstanding successes.

Experimenting with choreograph is a little more difficult logistically than, for example, painting a picture. A painter needs a canvas and paints, but choreographers need trained bodies and minds who are capable of interpreting their ideas. A dance does not exist before it is danced. Choreography involves long hours in the studio exploring possibilities, testing ideas, refining sequences, throwing out sections that do not work, and beginning again. It is a very public act of creation. No one knows how long a writer sat in front of a blank piece of paper before a paragraph was written; choreographers do not have that luxury. They must create within the framework of rehearsal schedules and performance dates, relying on the energy and talent of their dancers to do justice to their vision.

When the opportunity to see and take part in an outstanding repertory is limited, or missing altogether, the rules of the craft can be learned. Colleges offer courses in choreography in which its tenets can be explored. Artistically, composing a dance is very much like composing a picture. The painter uses line, texture, and color; the choreographer uses line, motion, and dynamics. The intent of both is the same — to create a composition that will please, move, or stimulate the viewer and challenge the dancer.

Choreographic experimentation is costly. Ballet-company directors are often reluctant to entrust an inexperienced choreographer with the production of a ballet, primarily because of the commitment of the dancers' time and energy. They also hesitate to cover all the adjunct costs of costuming and mounting the new production. There is a dearth of new choreographers in dance today because of this lack of opportunity to experiment, this license to fail. Modern dancers fare no better and often create their own opportunities to show their work. There are, however, state and federal grants that can help a young choreographer produce a concert. The local Arts Council is the first place to get information about the procedure.

If a dancer is driven to be a choreographer, she or he should take every opportunity to make dances, keep a quality video record of achievements, and choose venues where works will be seen, like the regional companies' festivals, or associate with other choreographers with the same goals.

History, Research, and Criticism

Writing about dance is a very rewarding option for former dancers, but one that requires an academic as well as a dancing background. Many dance critics, historians, and researchers writing today were originally dancers. However, the critic needs to have some experience with writing, preferably either English or journalism courses. Many dance critics start out writing reviews for their university paper.

The critic needs a wide knowledge of the dance repertory to write a good review, one that will not only describe the dance but place it in its historical context. I remember reading a review of *Cakewalk*, a ballet by Ruthanna Boris (b. 1918), in which Boris parodies ballets from different periods of history. The reviewer missed the references altogether, and thereby missed the opportunity to enlighten and educate the public.

If a dancer has an aptitude for writing, an ability to see and describe motion as well as intent and hidden meanings, dance criticism may well be an option to pursue. It is, however, a difficult field to enter, and a college education will greatly facilitate progress.

History and research are two fields that depend almost exclusively on an university affiliation. Writing dance books is not a lucrative profession (unless you write bestsellers); almost everyone in the field holds a teaching position. Research often demands a great deal of time and expenditure and is not readily available to people who are not affiliated with a university. Although grants are available to people who can present a good rationale for their interest in a particular area, these awards are most readily accessible to university professors.

Administration and Arts Management

Arts management has become a viable venue for former dancers because it requires a thorough knowledge of the arts world. However, the field is highly specialized and requires specific courses at a university or college. The responsibilities of the managing director of a dance company may include: staff and facility management; grant preparation and administration; budget development and oversight; negotiation of artists' contracts; and marketing. The managing director must also work closely with the artistic director in the strategic planning of the performance schedule. If a dancer is organized, has a good presence, and can juggle a variety of tasks — setting a touring schedule, talking to prospective donors, balancing a budget, and understanding the dynamics of a repertory — then, with training, she or he will probably be able to rise to the challenge of managing a dance company.

Therapy

Numerous schools offer training in massage therapy. Dancers make good massage therapists because they already have an appreciation of muscular functions and probably firsthand experience with the specific problems caused by pulled muscles, strains, sprains, and body aches. The training period for professional massage is of short duration. A year or two of intensive study will usually provide the skills necessary to become a massage therapist.

Dance-movement therapy, on the other hand, requires a background in psychology. Goucher College in Maryland, Hunter College in New York, U.C.L.A., and Columbia College in Chicago, among others, offer excellent programs in dance-movement therapy. This is a growing field, and it has much to offer to people who are interested in extending their dance knowledge into a fascinating area of healing.

Production, Lighting, and Design

Theatrical technical production includes many specialties, but most people in this field have a background in visual arts and design. Many universities offer production programs that provide an opportunity for hands-on experience in designing, mounting, and running a show. A dance background can be a stepping-stone, as it provides an appreciation for specific dance concerns in both lighting and costume designing.

Video

If one wishes to enter the media world from the dance world, the primary interest will probably be in recording dance. A fascinating field that has as yet no fixed boundaries, recording can range from record-filming (putting a dance on film in order to facilitate later revivals) to artistic collaborations between a choreographer and a video artist, in which the camera is used as a means of expression.

Again, the technical aspects of the profession can be learned in both colleges and professional schools. Dancers entering the field bring to it their own particular vision, honed by years of exploring motion.

. . .

Former dancers can be found in a variety of professions: the law, anthropology, psychiatry, physical therapy, theatre production, video, acting, fine arts, teaching. Although dancers may feel that they are ill-prepared for any other work, dance training instills a highly developed sense of discipline that helps the artists achieve success in whatever field they choose.

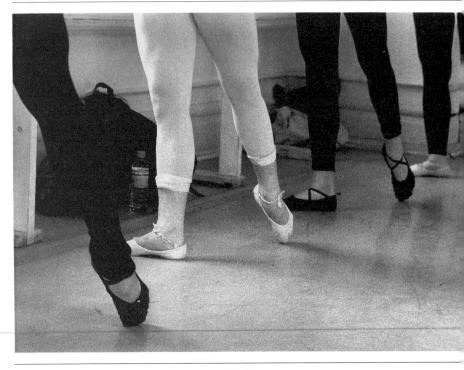

Students of the Chicago Academy for the Arts.
©1997 Mitchell Canoff

Parenting the Dancer

WE ARE ALWAYS a little surprised and somewhat delighted when our children show a dedication and a commitment that seems to us beyond their years. Parenting a dancer is not very different from parenting any talented child.

Children generally begin dance classes at an early age, when dance is, in most cases, an activity chosen by their parents. Sometimes, the children identify their desire. One mother commented to me, "When they do what they want, there is a healthy attitude toward the activity, and it has a maturing effect." She added, "It is a fascinating experience to be led by your child. It opened our lives. We do a lot of things that we would not have done, like going to dance concerts." Usually between the ages of nine and twelve, children begin to let their preference be known. Either the parent continues to drag the reluctant child to dance class for a few more years, or dance assumes a central position in the child's life.

Parents readily admit that parenting a dancing child is very demanding. One parent says, "If the child is committed, you must be committed too." This commitment begins with driving the child to and from class. "It takes a lot of time," another parent said. "There was a studio nearby, but it was not very good, so I drove her into town every day until she was sixteen and could drive." This mother admitted that she could not exercise much control over her daughter; "this was something that she wanted to do, and we tried to support and encourage her." After the child graduated from high school, she and her mother traveled through Europe auditioning. They were both under a lot of pressure, stayed in cheap hotels, and faced rejection on a daily basis. "I felt badly for her, was frustrated for her," the mother said. "You see the pain and bruises and wish there was something you could do."

Parents must be prepared to help their child cope with rejection. Dancers need a loving environment, because they may not get enough emotional support from their dance teacher, and often the dance teacher assumes a central role in shaping their self-image. If there are too many students in a class, or if the teacher is indifferent or abusive, the child will suffer. Another mother explained to me that she had taken her daughter out of the leading studio in her city because "the classes were too big, the students had little individual attention, and my daughter's self-esteem was suffering from the neglect." On the other hand, if the teacher is supportive and encouraging, the child will gain the confidence to strive in class. The mother of two dancing daughters commented, "We have not pushed them, but just helped them pursue what they want — gave them options, helped them stay motivated."

Making sure that their dancers eat the right food is another concern voiced by parents. Some children are very conscientious about their diet, but most need guidance. The mother of the two daughters said, "We have become more aware because of their needs. Our diet has more vegetables and protein in it, and very little fat. It is often a challenge to squeeze meals into the daily class schedule, because eating just before a class makes them feel bloated."

A young and dedicated dancer soon has to make some hard choices. Her or his social time is greatly curtailed, if not totally eliminated. One mother lamented, "When she was thirteen, all her friends deserted her. She started sobbing, then realized that she could not have it all." This mother was very upset, but she knew that she could not help. She had to let her daughter sort out her priorities. This experience had a maturing effect; the child became more self-reliant as her determination to become a dancer grew.

Most parents I have spoken to are acutely aware of the dangers of becoming a stage parent. "As a parent, you have to step back, not let your dreams get mixed up with the child's; not impose yours on hers. It has to be what she wants." When the child's motivation is not clear, there is always the danger that she or he will become a "pleaser." When this happens, a part of the personality is lost. Dancers then tend to see their worth only in terms of what other people think of them.

Symbiotic relationships are not uncommon between dancers and their mothers. These can be positive when the desires of the child concur with those of the mother, and there have been some legendary mother/daughter relationships. Tamara Toumanova (b. 1919), one of Balanchine's "baby ballerinas", was always accompanied by her mother; they were totally devoted to each other. Violette Verdy (b. 1933), was also devoted to her mother, who not only looked after Verdy's needs but mothered every member of the company. But these relationships can also have a dark side. One of the summer students at a school where I was once teaching had come from another state with her mother. Back home, the mother was working at the dance studio that the child attended. The mother watched every class and was always waiting with comments and corrections when her daughter came out of class. If you offered a cookie, the mother would say, "We're on a diet." She also stated, on one occasion, "We are allergic to milk" and "We go to bed early." The child was mostly silent, smiling, and compliant. The mother was making plans to move to the city to provide her daughter with the opportunity to study further with her summer teachers. Sometime later I received a letter from the mother: the child had broken her ankle, and they had returned to their hometown. The mother spoke of the injury as a terrible accident, but maybe this was the only way the daughter could make her wishes known to her domineering parent.

There is a fine line between support and coercion. The decision to become a dancer is made at a tender age; the aspiring dancer is hardly out of childhood when she or he commits to a way of life that she or he barely apprehends. That life is too hard to be imposed from the outside. Well-wishing parents who may be fulfilling their own unrealized dreams are unwittingly setting the scene for a disaster. Not only will their own dreams be dashed, but the child will suffer from a sense of guilt when she or he fails to achieve the dream for them both. The child's only recourse is often a dramatic, usually unconscious gesture that will free her or him of the situation and the guilt.

"Dance parents" generally tend to be highly involved in their children's lives. Certainly the time they commit to the activity of dance is considerable. As the student progresses through the technique, she or he must spend more and more time on it. It is often hard for the parent to maintain a healthy distance under these circumstances. But it is essential for parents to be able to distinguish between their hopes and aspirations and those of their child; they must provide the child enough room to mature and define her or his own goals.

Parents must also be prepared to make a financial commitment. Paying for classes and keeping the dancer supplied with shoes can strain a budget. You must remember that class is not a luxury; it is the very breath of the dancer. Without class, technique cannot be maintained and progress cannot be made. If your child is talented, most schools will provide a scholarship at best, a lower tuition rate at least. Don't be too proud to ask about financial assistance. The most important thing is for your child's training to go on uninterrupted.

An adequate supply of pointe shoes is also essential. All good artisans must have the required materials on hand to practice their craft, be it baking a cake, changing a tire, or knitting a sweater. Pointe shoes do not have a predictable lifespan; some last for months, others break after a few classes. If you cannot afford to buy several pairs at the same time, establish a relationship with the dance store to ensure that the size and type of shoe you need is always in stock.

Whether you have strong misgivings about your child pursuing a career in dance or you totally support this choice, you must remember that dance is more than a job; it is a way of life. To paraphrase Martha Graham, if one has been chosen by having been given certain attributes and longings, one must honor the gift.

I would like to conclude with the wise words of Mary Wigman in *The Language of Dance:*

Certainly we are able to do a great deal when it comes to molding and forming, to furthering and developing. But it is not in our power to create the often hotly desired talent. We are not even able to determine the degree and kind of talent. For if nature has not planted the fuel of artistic talent in man, no power, no desire, no will is able to ignite the torch to that flaming light in which the creative force can give of itself lavishly, in which the language of dance finds its heightened expression in a work of art and the dancer becomes the carrier and messenger of the art of dancing. Talent is a blessing. And so is the pedagogic talent in dance. Our task, however, lies in serving: to serve the dance, to serve the work, to serve man, and to serve life.

✢

Appendix

Aces Educational Center for the Arts (Public, Magnet)
55 Audubon St.
New Haven, Connecticut 06510
203-777-5451
Disciplines: Ballet, Modern Dance, Jazz, Tap.
Others, by semester. West African, Haitian

Douglas Anderson School for the Arts (Public)
2445 San Diego Road
Jacksonville, Florida 32207
904-346-5608
Disciplines: Ballet, Modern Dance, Jazz, Tap, Ethnic Dance,
Character Dance.
Electives: Ballet Variations, Choreography, Dance Production,
Men class.

The Bolles School (Private)
7400 San Jose Blvd.
Jacksonville, Florida 32217
Disciplines: Ballet, Modern Dance, Jazz, Tap, Musical Theatre,
Nutrition, Dance History, Injury Prevention, Choreography, Beg.
Kinesiology, Beg. Lighting.

Booker T. Washington Magnet High School (Public)
2001 West Fairview Ave.
Montgomery, Alabama 36108
334-268-3813
Disciplines: Ballet, Modern Dance, Jazz, Tap, Ethnic, Pointe,
Choreography.

Booker T. Washington School for the Performing and Visual Arts
(Public)
2501 Flora St.
Dallas, Texas 75201
214-720-7300
Disciplines Emphases: Ballet, Modern Dance.
Electives: Jazz, Tap, Musical Theatre, Dance History, Composition,
Laban Notation.

Cab Calloway School of the Arts (Public)
100 N. Dupont Rd.
Wilmington, Delaware 19807
302-651-2702
Disciplines: Movement according to students' needs.

Carver Center for Arts and Technology (Public)
938 York Rd.
Towson, Maryland 21204
410-887-2775
Disciplines: Ballet, Modern Dance, Laban Notation, Composition,
Modern Repertory, Dance History.

Carver Creative and Performing Arts Center (Magnet)
2001 W Fairview Ave.
Montgomery, Alabama 36108
334-269-3813
Disciplines: Ballet, Modern Dance, Jazz.

Cass Technical High School (Public)
2421 Second Ave.
Detroit, Michigan 48201
313-596-3900
Disciplines: Ballet, Modern Dance (Graham and Horton), Jazz,
Ethnic Dance, Tap, Choreography.

Center for the Arts (Public)
850 34th St. South
St, Petersburg, Florida 33711
813-893-5452
Disciplines: Ballet Modern Dance, Jazz, Tap, Character, Ethnic.

Center for the Arts and International Studies (Public)
9751 98th St. North
Largo, Florida 33777
813-545-6517
Disciplines: Ballet, Jazz.

Center for Creative Youth
Wesleyan University
327 High St.
Middletown, Connecticut 06067
860-685-3397

Chicago Academy for the Arts (Private)
1010 W. Chicago Ave.
Chicago, IL 60622
312-421-0202
Disciplines: Ballet, Modern Dance (Graham), Jazz, Pointe/
Variation, Men's Class, Dance History, Kinesiology, Body
Conditioning, Dance Survey.

Cooperative Arts & Humanities High School (Public)
444 Orange St.
New Haven, Connecticut 06511
203-946-5923
Disciplines: Ballet, Modern Dance, Jazz, Tap, Dance Foundations.

Denver School of the Arts (Public)
3240 Humbolot
Denver, Colorado 80205
303-764-6817
Disciplines: Ballet, Modern Dance, Jazz, Tap.

Duke Ellington High School for the Arts (Public)
3500 R St. NW
Washington, D.C. 20007
202-282-0123

Emerson Visual & Performing Arts (Public)
716 East 7th Ave.
Gary, Indiana 46402
219-886-6555
Disciplines: Ballet, Modern Dance, Jazz, Tap, Pointe, African
Dance, Choreography.

John L. Le Flore High School of Communication and Arts (Public)
700 Donald St.
Mobile, Alabama 36617
Disciplines: Ballet, Modern Dance, Jazz, Tap.

Fine Arts Center (Public)
1613 W Washington St.
Greenville, South Carolina 29601
Disciplines: Ballet, Modern Dance.

The Governor's School for the Arts (Public)
Old Dominion University
Norfolk, Virginia 23529
Disciplines: Ballet Modern Dance, Jazz, Tap, Ethnic Dance, Pilates
Method of Conditioning, Pas De Deux, Dance History, Anatomy
and Kinesiology, Rhythmic Analysis, Laban Notation, Movement
Analysis, Improvisation, Pointe, Variations, Repertory.

Greater Hartford Academy of the Arts (Public, Magnet)
235 Wethersfielf Ave.
Hartford, Connecticut 06114
860-522-8335
Disciplines: Ballet, Modern Dance, Dance History, Composition,
Improvisation, Repertory.
Electives: Tap, Jazz, Ethnic.

La Guardia High School of the Arts (Public)
100 Amsterdam Ave.
New York, New York 10023
212-496-0700
Ballet, Modern Dance, Survival Skills, Dance History, Acting for
Dancers, Choreography, Career Management, Character, Jazz,
Dance History, Tap.

High School for the Performing & Visual Arts (Public)
4001 Stanford St.
Houston, Texas 77006
713-942-1960
Disciplines: Ballet, Modern Dance, Jazz, Tap, Musical Theatre,
Dance History, Improvisation, Composition, Dance Photography.

Holland Hall School (Public)
5666 E 81st St.
Tulsa, Oklahoma 74137
918-481-1111
Disciplines: Modern Dance (Graham, Limon).

Idyllwild School of Music and the Arts (Private)
P.O. Box 38
Idyllwild, California 92549
909-659-2171
Disciplines: Ballet, Modern Dance, Jazz, Character, Tap, Composi-
tion, Anatomy/Kinesiology, Dance History, Music for Dancers.
Men's Class in Ballet, Modern, Jazz.

Interlochen Arts Academy (Private)
P.O. Box 199
Interlochen, Michigan 49643
616-276-7472
Disciplines: Ballet, Pointe, Character, Variations, Men Class,
Partnering, Modern, Jazz, Improvisation, Composition.

Martin Luther King, Jr., High School (Public)
3200 E Lafayette
Detroit, Michigan 48207
Disciplines: Modern.

Mercer County High School of the Performing Arts (Public)
1200 Old Trenton Rd.
Trenton, New Jersey 03690
Disciplines: Ballet, Modern Dance, Jazz, Composition, Dance
History, Acting, Voice.

Milwaukee High School of the Arts (Public)
2300 W. Highland Ave.
Milwaukee, Wisconsin 53233
414-933-1500
Disciplines: Ballet, Modern Dance, Jazz, Tap, African Dance,
Choreography.

New Orleans Center for Creative Arts (Public)
6048 Perrier St.
New Orleans, Lousiana 70118
504-899-0055
Disciplines: Ballet, Modern Dance, Jazz, Character, Dance History.

New Trier High School (Public)
385 Winnetka Ave.
Winnetka, Illinois 60093
847-446-7000
Disciplines: Modern Dance, Improvisation, Composition.

New World School of the Arts (Public)
300 NE 2nd Ave.
Miami, Florida 33132
305-237-3341
Disciplines: Ballet, Modern Dance, Jazz, Spanish Dance, African
Dance, Tap,Composition, Improvisation, Dance History,
Anatomy/Kinesiology, Injury Prevention, Dance Production,
Dance Criticism, Body Alignment, Performance.

North Atlanta School of the Arts (Public)
2875 Northside Dr.
Atlanta, Georgia 30305
Disciplines: Ballet, Modern Dance, Jazz.

Padua Academy (Private, Catholic, girls only)
905 N Broom St.
Wilmington, Delaware 19806
Disciplines: Ballet, Tap, Jazz.

Parkview Magnet High School (Public)
2501 Barrow Rd.
Little Rock, Arkansas 72204
501-228-3000
Disciplines: Ballet, Modern Dance, Jazz, Composition, Dance
History, Dance Ensemble.

Pinellas County Center for the Arts at Gibbs School (Public)
850 34th St. South
St. Petersburg, Florida 33711
Disciplines: Ballet (Vaganova), Modern Dance (Horton), Ethnic,
Music for Dancers, Anatomy and Injury Prevention, Stagecraft,
Dance History.

Dr. Phillips High School, Visual and Performing Arts Magnet
(Public)
6500 Turkey Lake Rd.
Orlando, Florida 32819
Ballet, Modern Dance, Jazz, Pointe, Lyrical, Tapage 1 ,
Improvisation.

Pittsburgh High School for the Creative and Performing Arts,
(Public)
925 Brushton Ave.
Pittsburgh, Pennsylvania 15208
412-247-7860
Disciplines: Ballet, Modern Dance, Jazz, Tap, Dance History,
Anatomy/Physiology

San Francisco School of the Arts (Public)
700 Font Blvd.
San Francisco, California 94132
415-469-4027
Disciplines: Ballet, Modern Dance, Folk, Afro-Asian Dance.

Saint Maria Goretti High School for Girls (Private, Catholic)
1736 South 10th St.
Philadelphia, Pennsylvania 18148
215-465-8437
Disciplines: Ballet, Tap, Jazz.

School for Creative and Performing Arts (Public)
1310 Sycamore St.
Cincinnati, Ohio 45210
513-632-5912
Disciplines: Ballet, Pointe, Partnering, Character, Modern Dance
(Graham).

Unionville High School, Arts Program (Public)
201 Town Centre Blvd.
Unionville
Ontario, Canada L3Y 4V8
416-479-2787
Disciplines: Ballet, Modern Dance, Jazz, Multicultural Dance,
Musical Theatre, Performance.

Walnut Hill School (Private)
12 Highland Street
Natick, Massachussets 01760
508-650-5020
Disciplines: Ballet, Pointe.

Youth Performing Arts School (Public)
1517 South Second St.
Louisville, Kentucky 40208
502-485-8355
Disciplines: Ballet, Modern Dance, Jazz.

IN CANADA

Canterbury High School
Ottawa, Ontario

Claude Watson Arts Program
New York, Ontario

Ecole Secondaire publique De La Salle
Ottawa, Ontario
Disciplines: Ballet, Modern Dance.

Etobicoke School for the Arts
Etobicoke, Ontario

Hamilton-Wentworth Catholic School Arts Center
Hamilton, Ontario

Langley Fine Arts School
Fort Langley, British Columbia

Lincoln County School of Performing Arts
Niagara-on-the-Lake, Ontario

Mayfield Secondary School
Brampton, Ontario

Peel Regional Arts Program
Mississauga
(Arts in education program rather than pre-professional
training.)

Sudbury Secondary School, Sudbury

Unionville High School Art York Programme
Unionville, Ontario

Victoria Composite High School
Edmonton, Alberta

IN AUSTRALIA

Newtown High School of the Performing Arts (Public)
P.O. Box 785
Newtown, NSW 2042
Australia 011-612-95191657

Selected Bibliography

Anderson, Jack. *Ballet and Modern Dance: A Concise History.* Princeton, NJ: Princeton Book Company, 1986. A very useful and entertaining book offering an overview of dance history. Short profiles at the end of the book provide a "Who's Who" of dance-world personalities.

Barringer, Janice, and Sarah Schlesinger. *The Pointe Book: Shoes, Training and Technique.* Princeton, NJ: Princeton Book Company, 1990. The most complete treatise on what it takes to dance on your toes. Includes a history of the dancer's rise onto pointe.

Beaumont, Cyril. *Michel Fokine and His Ballets.* Brooklyn, NY: Dance Horizons, 1981.

Brown, Jean Morrison, ed. *The Vision of Modern Dance.* Princeton, NJ: Princeton Book Company, 1979. Essays by the pioneers of modern dance.

Buckle, Richard. *In Search of Diaghilev.* London Sidgwick Publishers, 1955. Mr. Buckle is the foremost expert on Diaghilev.

Cohen, Selma Jean, ed. *Dance As a Theatre Art: Source Readings in Dance History from 1581 to the Present.* 2nd ed. Princeton, NJ: Princeton Book Company, 1991.

Demidov, Alexandre. *Russian Ballet Past and Present.* New York: Doubleday, 1977.

Duncan, Isadora. *My Life.* New York. Liveright, 1927. For a less subjective account of Duncan's life, see Victor Seroff's *The Real Isadora.* New York: Dial, 1971.

Ellfeldt, Lois. *From Magic to Art*. Dubuque, IA: Wm. C. Brown, 1976. A comprehensive look at dance through the ages. Includes enlightening quotes from critics, teachers, dancers, and choreographers.

Feldenkrais, Moshe. *Awareness through Movement*. New York: Harper & Row, 1972.

Fleming, Gladys Andrews, ed. *Children's Dance*. Washington, DC: AAHPERD Press, 1973. Recommends dance activities for children from the ages of three to twelve.

Friedman, Philip, and Gail Eisen. *The Pilates Method of Mental and Physical Conditioning*. New York: Warner Books, 1981.

Gordon, Suzanne. *Off Balance*. New York: Pantheon, 1983. A brutally honest account of the dancing life in New York.

Graham, Martha. *Blood Memory*. New York: Doubleday, 1991. Graham's autobiography.

Hammond, Sandra Noll. *Ballet Basics* (1974); *Beyond the Basics* (1982). CA: Mayfield Publishing, Palo Alto. Both books provide easy-to-read guidelines to technique as well as general information about the dance world.

Horosko, Marian, and Judith R. F. Kupersmith, M.D. *The Dancer's Survival Manual*. New York: Harper & Row, 1987. Covers everything from diet to plastic surgery.

Humphrey, Doris. *The Art of Making Dances*. Princeton, NJ: Princeton Book Company, 1990. Practical guide for would-be choreographers.

Kirkland, Gelsey, and Greg Lawrence. *Dancing on my Grave*. New York: Doubleday, 1986. A heartrending account of the life of one of America's greatest ballerinas.

Kirstein, Lincoln. *Portrait of Mr. B*. New York: Viking, 1984. A biographical essay on George Balanchine with numerous photos.

Latimer, Jane Evans. *Living Binge Free*. Boulder, CO: Livingquest, 1988.

Laws, Kenneth. *The Physics of Dance*. New York: Schirmer Books, 1984. Dance movement explained scientifically.

Mara, Thalia. *First Steps in Ballet; Second Steps in Ballet; Third Steps in Ballet; On Your Toes*. Princeton, NJ: Princeton Book Company, 1987. Perfect reading for young dancers.

Martin, John. *The Modern Dance*. Brooklyn, NY: Dance Horizons 1965. A series of lectures, originally given in 1931 and 1932, outlining the philosophy of early modern-dance pioneers.

Paskevska, Anna. *Both Sides of the Mirror: The Science and Art of Ballet*.

Brooklyn, NY: Dance Horizons, 1981. 2nd ed. by Princeton Book Company, 1992.

———. *Ballet. From the First Plie to Mastery.* Pennington, NJ: Princeton Book Company, 1990.

Reynolds, Nancy, ed. *The Dance Catalog: A Complete Guide to Today's World of Dance.* New York: Harmony Books, 1979

Rone, Elvira and Fernau Hall. *Olga Preobrazhenskaya: a Portrait.* New York: Marcel Dekker, 1978. A loving biography of the great ballerina.

Shook, Karel. *Elements of Classical Ballet Technique.* Brooklyn, NY: Dance Horizons, 1977. A treatise on the classical technique as practiced at the Dance Theatre of Harlem in New York.

Solomon, Ruth, Sandra C. Minton, and John Solomon, eds. *Preventing Dance Injuries.* American Alliance for Health, Physical Education, Recreation and Dance, 1990.

Sorrel, Walter. *The Dance through the Ages.* London, Grosset-Dunlap, 1967.

Spignesi, Angelyn. *Starving Women.* Dallas, TX: Spring Publications, 1983.

Stransky, Judith, and Robert B. Stone. *The Alexander Technique: Joy in the Life of Your Body.* New York: Beaufort Books, 1981.

Vaganova, Agrippina. *Basic Principles of Classical Ballet: Russian Ballet Technique.* New York: Dover Publications, 1946.

Vincent, L.M., M.D. *Competing with the Sylph: Dancers and the Pursuit of the Ideal Body Form.* 2nd ed. Princeton, NJ. Princeton Book Company, 1980. Should be required reading for every aspiring dancer.

Wigman, Mary. *The Language of Dance.* Trans. by Walter Sorrell. Middletown, CT: Wesleyan University Press, 1966. Descriptions of the dances that Wigman composed.

Wright, Stuart. *Dancer's Guide to Injuries of the Lower Extremities.* Cornwall Books, Cranbury N.J. 1985).

Index